FLY TO THE BOARDROOM

Your Essential Guide to Getting on a Board

STACEY DANIEL

First published by Busybird Publishing 2020

ISBN
Print: 978-1-925949-69-8
Ebook: 978-1-925949-70-4

Cover photo: Bruce Hemburrow
Back cover photo: Justin Cooper
Cover design: Busybird Publishing
Layout and typesetting: Busybird Publishing
Illustrations: Stacey Daniel

Busybird Publishing
2/118 Para Road
Montmorency, Victoria
Australia 3094
www.busybird.com.au

Disclaimer
This book is intended to be an easy-to-read introduction to boards and board work. The contents of the book are based on the author's personal experience and research, and her opinions may differ to views expressed by others. This book is general information only and should not be relied upon for legal or professional advice.

Dedication

To my husband and children, for supporting me on this journey.

To the many people who make significant personal, career and financial sacrifices to raise and elevate others.

To those who enrich the world and make a difference.

CONTENTS

FOREWORD

I am honoured to have been asked by Stacey to provide a foreword for this engaging and informative book, *Fly to the Boardroom*. I have been fortunate to work with Stacey in her capacity as a non-executive director and admire her diversity in thinking, passion and approach to board work, governance and sustainability.

I value the important contribution that boards and their committees make to organisations and communities. Today we operate in a constantly changing and challenging environment. Boards increasingly need directors with a broader range of insights and perspectives on issues affecting their organisations. It is pleasing to see greater diversity and talent entering the boardroom to help strengthen the outcomes of board decision-making.

My own non-executive director journey started seven years ago when I joined the board of an environmental enterprise, Greening Australia. Subsequently, I was appointed to a series of boards across different sectors responsible for alpine resorts, TAFE and higher education, and the regulation of architects. My roles in boardrooms as a non-executive director have included fulfilling positions such as chair, a general board member and a subcommittee member.

Stacey has compiled an insightful, light-hearted and easy-to-understand guide for aspiring and new non-executive directors seeking to better understand the workings of boards. These include both the process by which directors gain a seat at the board table and the governance arrangements around board and committees.

The book has been written in a conversation style and is infused with stories of Stacey's board experiences along the way. Although introductory in nature, its purpose and content will particularly help anyone curious about a board career and can also assist those early in their boardroom progression.

For those who believe a board appointment is out of reach, this book will show you a way forward. I encourage you to take the journey from cover to cover.

Arianne Rose
Chair and Non-Executive Director

Introduction

Welcome to the world of boards, committees and directorships. A world which is powerful and full of opportunity. A world where boards can achieve great things and you too can contribute, drive change and make a difference.

Boards are a place of discussion, debate and decision-making. They set directions, make plans, determine policies and guide outcomes. Boards and their members are custodians of the future, with the ability to progress proactively. Being a director, partaking in and contributing to deliberations that generate sustainable outcomes, is meaningful, rewarding and fulfilling.

No matter what industry or sector, having a seat at the boardroom table is a privilege and an honour. Whether your purpose is for enhancing business, the community, the environment or some other reason, it is an exciting proposition to bring all you've got to the board table. Your knowledge, skills and attributes – everything that makes you who you are – can help drive future directions and generate value and benefit.

This book was inspired by people like you, who share a desire to apply themselves to make a difference. It recognises that you, like me, may not necessarily have been a high-profile executive looking for a post-executive board role or career, but rather are a committed and competent operator with your own unique set of attributes. Someone who can see and command a way to make things better.

When I first realised my interest in boards, I was drawn to the idea of strategic decision-making and better outcomes, however I hadn't considered a board career. Yet upon reflection by following my heart, I had actually developed an accidental board career, and an early one.

My board journey to date has been exciting and enjoyable. I have fulfilled board roles for public sector authorities, not-for-profit organisations and a peak industry body, as well as advising boards and directors across all sectors, including private industry.

Many people, especially women, have asked me how I got onto boards. The more times I was asked this question, the more I realised I had to share my board story. As living proof, I demonstrate that the same opportunity exists for you, and this book can help you get there.

In sharing my story, I provide insights and information about boards. I also provide a blueprint for how you can also get a board role, gain some boardroom presence and start a board career too.

I draw on the benefit of my board experience, consolidate steps and streamline a process to help you focus, saving you valuable time, energy, effort and cost.

This is my gift to you. A source of insight, information and inspiration. Something that is educational, thought-provoking and practical for your own tangible outcomes. I wanted to offer a useful, easy-to-read and easy-to-digest book. Something which is straight-forward and enables you to design your own journey to the boardroom. My ultimate aim is to take you on a flying trip to the boardroom!

In the upcoming chapters I draw on my experience to help demystify the world of boards for you. I will help you gain knowledge, understanding and confidence about boards and being a director. You will learn about opportunities most suited to you, new tools to help guide you, what you need to do, and how to overcome barriers to make a board position a reality.

With clarity, you can expect to feel relieved, excited and confident. Most importantly, you'll be able to feel the sense of fulfilment as you travel the path to becoming a director, en route to the boardroom and your own board career.

I will teach you, guide you, challenge you, reward you and hopefully amuse you along the way! This is a light-hearted introduction to boards and a relatable structure to put your best foot forward. A simple, systematic, no-pressure process to build and develop you personally as well as professionally.

You will go on a transformational journey of personal exploration, discovery and preparation to board the right flight to the right destination. The duration of this journey will be as short or as long as you wish.

The timeframe is up to you. If now is not the right time for you, you can do the preparations and return to it later. This process is only a guide and your success will be reflected in your own personal drive, energy and effort. Like a horse to water, I can only lead you – the rest is up to you.

If you have the curiosity, a desire or a fire in your belly, there has never been a better time to consider being on a board or committee – especially if you are female.

I believe boards and committees can change the world, and so can you! The future is now and the steps you take today are an investment for tomorrow and beyond.

This book was written out of a passion to help individuals, directors and boards better position themselves for better outcomes. This book forms part of a holistic approach, complemented by templates, resources, courses and events available for anyone wishing to accelerate, elevate and fly high! Details of these are available at the back of this book and online at **www.boardpresence.com.au**.

With that said, let's commence your new journey, start your new story and create a new chapter for you. Let's take you on a flying trip as you *Fly to the Boardroom*! Enjoy your flight!

1

NEW HORIZONS

'Congratulations! You've been appointed to the board.'

Wouldn't that be the greatest? Hearing those words? Goal: To get on a board … tick!

It wasn't quite like that, but near enough. A number of years ago, I was enjoying a well-earned break for a week on a tropical island in Queensland. After taking my young children for a swim in the pool, I laid down on the couch for a rest. I was half asleep when the phone rang. Not thinking clearly and in a daze, I answered the call. The words I heard were, 'Hi Stacey, you've been appointed'.

Where else would you rather be to receive such exciting news? I couldn't believe it! I was trying to comprehend the fact that this was a reality. This was a pivotal moment. I had literally gone from bored to board in an instant. I was now suddenly a director on the board of an organisation responsible for a substantial asset base and significant annual revenue.

This could happen to you too. You're an intelligent person, right? And no doubt you've got good skills and perspectives. You're someone who likes a challenge, likes to contribute and has a growing desire to make a difference, yes? The only problem is that you're not sure how or where to start when it comes to boards. If this is what you're thinking, have no fear, you're not alone!

Maybe you've heard about boards and are eager to know more? You may be unsure of how they operate or have some other concerns which are holding you back? Simply, it may be a case of 'I. Need. Help!'

I want to help you! I'd like to empower you and help transform your thinking and mindset. I'd like to also provide you with knowledge and understanding, and offer you the right tools to build your confidence about boards.

I'm going to share with you a streamlined process to help guide you through what can be a difficult journey to navigate. If you're curious about boards, or considering a board role or board career, it can be easy to lose direction. You can be at risk of wasting plenty of time, effort and even hard-earned money trying to head to a destination which isn't going to suit you. Or you may find yourself trying to travel without the right documentation.

To focus your time and energies effectively, I'm keen to unravel some of the mysteries or worries you may have about boards and highlight the real opportunities for you. In this first chapter, you will be exposed to a whole new world where you can open your mind to the array of possibilities and overcome any negative or limiting beliefs.

In this awakening phase, you will gain an appreciation of what boards are, how they've changed, the opportunities available to you and how you can play a role. You will understand your short and long-term prospects and why now is the perfect time to consider a board role or career.

A whole new adventure awaits. You're going on a journey of breaking down barriers, exploring new horizons and discovering new destinations. Allow your mind to be calm, relax your soul and be guided on some of the key essentials about boards.

Boards

Firstly, let's cover some of the basics: background, terminology and definitions. What is a board? What does it do? What is its purpose for existing?

According to the *Cambridge Dictionary*, a board is defined as a 'group of people who are responsible for controlling and organising a company or organisation' (Cambridge University Press, 2019).

Boards are made up of individuals assigned with administering an entity, who make important decisions and provide oversight of an organisation's governance and activities. They have a role and duty in making decisions today for tomorrow, whether that tomorrow is in one week, one month, one year, ten years, thirty years or longer.

Boards may also be referred to as board of directors, committees, councils or trusts, for example. Essentially, they have similar roles of responsibility and a duty of oversight, direction and decision-making, although there can be differences between these types of boards.

Terminology associated with boards can vary across business sectors. Despite the various types of boards, these terms are sometimes used interchangeably, however they can actually have different meanings depending on the nature of the business and the purpose of the board.

More confusing for new players is the terminology which describes board members and those who sit on the board. Again, there are different titles often used interchangeably, including non-executive directors, board members, members, councillors, committee members and trustees, amongst others.

Board members are generally known as non-executive directors (NEDs). Non-executive directors do not work within the business but have a strategic and decision-making responsibility only. Whereas executive directors are those who are involved within the organisation responsible for operational work and implementing the strategy to deliver outcomes.

Gaining a seat at the board table is a job. A job with the role of gathering information, asking questions, learning other perspectives, assessing information and making decisions. Whilst being a NED may not be a job in the traditional sense, it is the role of a board member to contribute just as you would as an employee, consultant or contractor engaged to deliver a service.

Interestingly, like many things, boards have evolved over time. Prior to the 1980s, boards were rarely seen and only heard of by those internal to the organisation who had to hear what they had to say (Gillies & Leblanc, 2005). Boards had little presence in the community and despite legal responsibilities, played a limited role. Corporate governance was not well practiced. These days, with greater focus on duties and governance, the board and its directors play a much greater role.

Also evolving are the seats around the board table. Over the years, they have often been filled by those with significant business experience to enable an organisation to draw on what is deemed the broadest base of insight. As a result, boards have been accused of appointing too many executives and post-executive retirees, often males and older in age.

This approach to board member appointments has neglected insight from other facets of the community and life experience. The tendency to appoint similar people to boards has often led to an imbalance of community representation, therefore not reflecting the characteristics for whom decisions are being made.

Boards will continue to further evolve as the world changes. The boards of today are expected to stand up, be seen and have greater presence as they play an important role within society. In a world where social and environmental issues are expected to be addressed, there is real opportunity to add value and make a difference by being on a board.

Boards of tomorrow

Boards can change the world for the better. As collective decision-makers, they have the opportunity to influence and achieve great outcomes. They can advance progress by setting reasonable goals and targets, establishing a positive organisational tone and culture, formulating good strategies and plans, introducing contemporary policies and procedures, solving problems with new solutions and advocating on broader issues. The chance for change is endless.

Within the community, across government, amongst private businesses and amidst large corporate organisations, there are many board and committee roles to be filled.

As the population increases, many new businesses and entities continue to emerge. With organisational activities continuing to grow, one can only expect an increase in the number of non-executive director roles available in years to come.

Successful boards of tomorrow will gain and maintain the confidence of their stakeholders by demonstrating social responsibility. The 'Edelman Trust Barometer Global Report' is an annual snapshot of trust and credibility across different countries, industries and segments of society.

Results from public surveys conducted in late 2019, highlight that the general population of Australia continues to distrust institutions (Edelman, 2020). There is a desire to improve societal conditions and there is an expectation for business to lead that change, particularly Chief Executive Officers (CEOs), hence the importance of an effective board to whom the CEO reports.

There have been disappointing and perhaps epic corporate failures in recent times both in Australia and internationally. Royal commissions, investigations and court proceedings have uncovered multiple examples of poor practices and performance. Some of these examples extend to the boardroom, further highlighting the need to update approaches at board level.

It is the responsibility of current and future board members to bring honesty to the boardroom and ensure good practices are upheld. I believe there is a growing demand for directors who can appropriately manage other people's money, not waste public or shareholders' funds, use time effectively, and add value both now and in the future.

Perhaps there is also an increased desire for board members with greater grounding and connection. Directors with a broader sense of community understanding, integrated business and life skills, and a genuine interest in making the best decisions for others.

You may have noticed or experienced this yourself: society demanding leaders and decision-makers who fit this description, who are informed and reflect the community's social values, morals and ethics.

This refers to not just the short-term and foreseeable period ahead, but for the long-term. Those with a greater sense of future impact and equitable value for all generations; perhaps those who think outside the box or over the horizon. This future-focus is what society needs to plan for and make decisions about.

Sometimes it can take multiple perspectives together to help see this far. Often it is the imaginative, creative and innovative people who help challenge the norm. Those who question the unknown future and guide the way to better solutions and more informed decisions. Those not constrained by limited mindsets or boundaries in possibilities.

These people are often known as deep thinkers. They offer significant insight and benefit to business and society as a result of their ability. Do you know someone who fits this description?

To highlight the attributes of tomorrow's non-executive director, a post from The Governance Institute UK lists some essential qualities of a non-executive director (Evan, 2016). Those being:

- Big picture thinker: who thinks strategically and critically without getting caught up in the detail.
- Governance knowledge: who has an understanding of the relevant legal frameworks and responsibilities to enhance the board's outcomes.
- Independent mindset: who has the capability to be objective, set aside issues and interests, to focus on what's really needed.
- Ambassador potential: who is able to be a face and representative of the organisation.
- Energy and commitment: who works to be effective and up-to-date.

A world of opportunity

With inclusion and diversity on the global agenda, we are seeing a growing recognition of the value of these broader viewpoints around the board table. This helps to understand issues, as well as drive organisational outcomes and business benefits.

Research has highlighted that companies with the most ethnically and culturally diverse boards worldwide are 43% more likely to experience higher profits (McKinsey & Company, 2018).

As a result of awareness and advocacy, boards are shifting to a greater presence of board members with diverse skills and perspectives.

Those from traditionally under-represented backgrounds with value-adding views are increasingly being sought and appointed to boards, highlighting the growing appreciation of broader input into issues and solutions.

A smart board will have a good mix of strengths to reflect its stakeholders and shareholders; referred to as a 'skills-based board'. Such a board will aim to optimise the quality of its collective leadership, decision-making and ultimate outcomes.

There are various interpretations of diversity. In the context of this book, diversity refers to individual offerings of skills, knowledge or attributes, including but not limited to, technical expertise, personal experience, age, gender, ability and culture.

In recognition of this, significant advocacy and movement has taken place across all industries and sectors to increase female representation at board and executive levels to at least represent women in society. Crazy, huh? Who would have thought such a thing was a good idea?!

In recent years, there has been a push and progression towards improving gender balance on boards. This is primarily due to directives and mandates set by industries, organisations and governments around the world to increase the proportion of females on boards.

Monitoring over this time has seen an increase in Australia of women appointed to boards in the public sector as well as the ASX200 (Australia's top 200 companies) – from 20% females on ASX200 boards in 2015 to reaching the 2018 goal of 30% at the end of November 2019 (AICD, 2019).

Whilst this emphasis on gender balance is a positive improvement, there remains further work to be undertaken to achieve inclusion of other under-represented groups across society.

Given changes in legislation and promotion of anti-discrimination across all aspects of life, the potential exists for inclusive directives to be applied to other forms of diversity on boards.

Interestingly, until recently, if you were a young non-executive director like I was when first appointed, chances are most of your mates didn't understand! At the time, many of my friends had little knowledge of boards, their purpose, role or function, as there were few young board members.

When I was appointed to my first public sector board, I was the youngest by about 15 years, and then by about 20 years on my next appointment. I felt a little out of place but appreciative of the opportunity to voice my view and opinions. I was able to represent my market segment by providing insight on issues others weren't aware of.

I appreciated contributing to and making decisions for both the short and long-term. I brought to my boards: a female perspective, a younger perspective, a young family's perspective and a professional perspective. I also brought along an engineer's solutions-mind, an understanding of sustainability, a social conscience, and a sense of future risk and impact.

I was pleased to see diversity being embraced and an appreciation of what different perspectives can bring to the board table, which ultimately benefits stakeholders and society in general.

Having previously worked in male-dominated industries such as mining and engineering, gender imbalances hadn't concerned me. However I was thrilled to see a transition to a broader representation of board members from different backgrounds. About five years after one of my first board appointments, I was joined by others my age, both female and male.

What I noticed around the board table though was a balance of viewpoints which better reflected society.

I observed a greater connection between the board membership and the target market and customers for whom the board was making decisions. As a result, board meetings were far more interesting, enjoyable and progressive.

The boardroom became vibrant and an environment of enriched discussion, healthy debate and contemporary decision-making. A reasonable assumption to think – that a board with a rich blend of knowledge, experience and skill can more effectively draw on the past, operate for the present and prepare for the future.

It is essential to take from this the fact that the world of boards has changed and will continue to change; and that there has been and continues to be a shift towards boards and committees that are expertise-based and skills-based.

Some boards suffer from limiting, outdated organisational rules and constitutions, whilst others are adapting to the 21st century societal and business landscape.

Smart boards are breaking the moulds to go beyond their traditional catchment of potential board members in order to increase their independent representation, opening the doors to a more diversified approach. This is a move which is enhancing their board, organisational outcomes and ultimate success.

I recently worked with a board considering this exact point. This well-needed community organisation was on a steady decline and had to take a good hard look at themselves to work out how to sustain their service.

To their credit, they took the recommendations, stepped up and made some significant decisions to future-proof themselves in order to continue delivering services to their beneficiaries.

Your opportunity

Given all of this, it might be fair to say that in the past you may have developed a perspective that boards are exclusive and conservative. Yes? Maybe this involved an impression that boards are reserved for other people, perhaps people who have achieved certain corporate goals or executive milestones? You may have held a view that boards are rigid, unfriendly and unapproachable? I'm here to tell you that this is not the case!

Perceptions, real or imaginary, can be brutal and debilitating. Ideally you want to overcome any mindset barriers caused by such limiting thoughts or beliefs so you can achieve your board goals!

Throughout this blueprint, I'll show you how to overcome perceived barriers. You might be thinking, 'But I'm only a …' or 'But I've been a stay-at-home parent for the past few years …' or 'But I'm not in management or an executive'.

Just because you're not retired or haven't been a high-flying executive doesn't mean you can't have a seat at the board table or have a fulfilling board career.

Perhaps you're like me, where as a result of some life experiences, your career journey has been somewhat unconventional. Your experience and insights to date haven't necessarily developed via traditional managerial or executive roles. Do you know anyone who may have found themselves in a similar situation?

In my case, a number of people saw my attributes and capabilities which gave them confidence that I would be a suitable non-executive director for a board. As a result, I was fortunate to have been appointed multiple times and each time by different people responsible for the appointment process.

I'm not one for giving false hope and promising that it will be the same for you. But my message for you is that if I can do it, you can too in some way, shape or form. Our work or life journeys may vary but there's no reason why you can't also contribute and experience something similar.

I'm also trying to point out that it's simply the difference between individual career pathways. None are any better than another, but rather each person is equally rich in strength and offering.

The reality is that it's a case-by-case situation depending on the specific organisation and the needs of the board at the time. In a world where creativity and entrepreneurship are thriving, and portfolio careers or multiple jobs are increasing, it's not unreasonable to expect to see more non-executive directors from unconventional backgrounds and careers offering unique insights and perspectives.

Might there be merit in this? Think about it this way: some people have natural boardroom skills and are able to comfortably form part of a collective group. Others have or may appear to have all the relevant business skills but are actually very limited in boardroom skills.

The reality is that we all have a set of skills, attributes and capabilities which differ from the next person. Irrespective of how our perspectives are derived, whether through personal or professional experience, we are equipped with a deep knowledge and understanding of topics. This makes us valuable amongst a collective skill mix on a board.

You may have little or no qualifications, yet have developed specialised skills in a particular field. Or you may have a unique, natural hidden talent, or specific insight or ability which is highly prized and value-adding?

If this is the case, gain a clear understanding of your expertise and how your insight can best be applied. You can draw on these attributes, not only to make a positive contribution to a board, but to fulfil your own potential and gain a great sense of personal satisfaction.

What if you had the opportunity to generate and create great positive change on a board? Perhaps through being involved in developing short and long-term strategic plans, financial planning, appointing a CEO, reviewing organisational performance, and/or developing a new product or service.

Or maybe through influencing key external matters, such as legislative reform, State strategy or public policy, for example. I did, and not only was it interesting, I was making a better tomorrow.

The opportunities for you to bring all you've got to the board table and make a difference are endless. The key is knowing the best options which lie ahead of you.

Imagine having the chance to drive valuable benefits, reduce negative impacts, improve quality or increase rates of return – whatever it is that is important to you, your family and community. Perhaps you want to increase social outcomes, protect the environment and improve business?

Whatever the drive, this is the beginning of your board journey! Your flying opportunity to the boardroom which extends along pathways over the horizon, into the future, possibly to other board positions.

Beyond the horizon may be chair roles, leadership opportunities, other decision-making roles or an entrepreneurial journey. You might go to places you've not even thought of yet, achieving personal goals, creating a future and adding value to what's most important to you and those around you.

Your journey begins

The Macquarie Dictionary describes opportunity as 'an appropriate or favourable time or occasion' (Macquarie University, 1997).

Hopefully you now understand why it is perfect timing for you to consider a board role or board career. Given movements towards greater diversity on boards, there has never been a better time to take action and throw your hat in the ring.

I hope you also now know and appreciate that boards and committees are no longer exclusive and are something anyone can consider. Of course, without denying that there are qualifiers, depending on the requirements of the board.

Most importantly, you've been able to dispel misconceptions and limiting beliefs, e.g. the thought that board roles are for certain people. Understand that there are many board and committee positions for those who have travelled less traditional career pathways or feel they don't align with the traditional image of a NED.

No matter where you are in the world, no matter what time, with the right mindset, every moment represents an opportunity. Seize it! Recognise this is your chance, your pivotal point, to change future direction, to follow or create a new path.

Sometimes we can experience barriers and busyness in our lives that cause us to miss turning points. Perhaps you've been too afraid, too overwhelmed or too engaged with being a parent or carer, entrepreneur, community leader, a worker or even an executive. This is how life unfolds and perhaps intuitively it just wasn't the right time for a board role, but with a heightened board-awareness and a new mindset, now may be the right time.

In picking up this book you already have a degree of awareness of boards, the power of boards and the potential of board membership. You may be a curious, aspiring, emerging, new, established (or a disconnected) NED, or perhaps even an accidental NED?

You may not yet be clear in your mind what the next opportunity is or what you're actually seeking. If that's the case, there's no need to worry; you're not alone in your thinking and that's okay! Most importantly you understand that this is a starting point and many others feel the same way you do.

To put your phase in context, it is helpful to understand the overall journey of a non-executive director. It looks something like Figure 1.

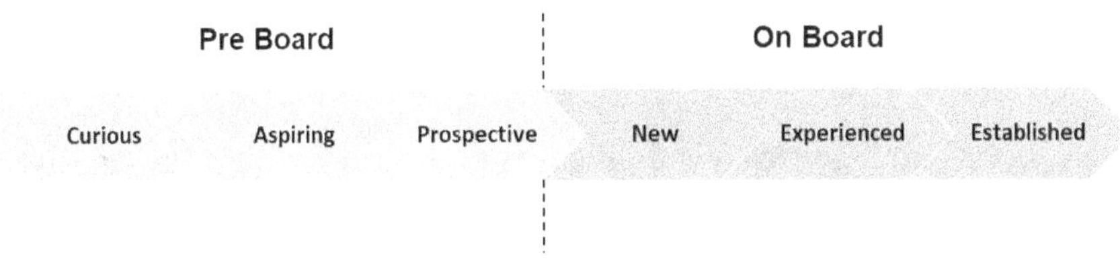

Figure 1: A director's journey

To give you some insight into these phases as a director, I like to describe them in the following way:

- Curious: This is a stage of uncertainty. You may know of boards but are not exactly sure what they do or if they're something you can get involved with.

- Aspiring: This is a phase of awareness. You know what boards are and what they do. You know you want to get on one and contribute to creating great outcomes but don't yet feel ready to step up.

- Prospective: This phase is about preparation and positioning. You know about boards, want to be on one and are ready to take on a board role. You are actively seeking board opportunities.

- New: This stage recognises you as duly appointed to a board. At this point, you have limited board experience, perhaps only on one board.

- Experienced: This is a phase which acknowledges that you have undertaken a number of years sitting on and contributing to one or more boards.
- Established: This stage recognises your diverse board experience and substantial practise as a director for many years across different types of boards.

There are many variables and these simplified stages are intended to reflect the life of a board career. They indicate a director's journey so you can identify where you might fit and what's ahead. You may have even already jumped the first few stages!

Your board journey may be like other journeys we take in life. Sometimes we don't always know where they're going to take us, but we instinctively know it's in a direction we want to head. That feeling when there's an urge or an attraction, that sense of being drawn towards something. You know it, yes? Try not to overthink it. Be open-minded to new ideas and go with the flow.

For many years, my husband and I had a desire to travel Australia. We always wanted to see more of our homeland, especially the northwest and central part of the country. We were keen to explore new places and have adventures we hadn't experienced before.

Seven years ago, our children were young and we had flexibility around our commitments. The time was right that we could respond to our instinctive urge, follow our hearts, and commit to taking that trip we'd always dreamt about.

To make sure it was the experience of a lifetime, we prepared well. We took about seven months, twice as long as our trip, researching and planning our adventure. We considered timeframes, specific destinations and experiences, seasons and weather, roads and accessibility, accommodation, food and gear.

Equipped with our new information, we confirmed our travel dates, made necessary bookings and purchased other essentials. With one step at a time and packing one item at a time, we were ready for our three-and-a-half-month trip to some of the most remote places in Australia!

Once we left, it was one kilometre at a time in the direction we wanted to go, travelling through South Australia, Western Australia and the Northern Territory.

We had the most amazing trip any family could have and created a lifetime of memories that could never be repeated. Whilst there were some hiccups, these only added to our adventure and experience. Each one of us gained perspectives on life that only a trip like that could give.

Having had so much fun, we decided to set off again on other adventures throughout the country. Our other trips included Australia's east coast and Fraser Island, outback Queensland and Cape York, and Tasmania.

Planning a new trip or venturing on a board career can be just like preparing for any other journey!

The new horizon

If your mind kicks in with 'I don't think I could get on a board', then I say keep reading! There are many opportunities out there. This framework will help you work systematically through any fears or worries you have.

Maybe you're concerned there's a whole lot about boards you don't understand? Did you know everything when you started that new job or that business? Probably not, but you started somewhere and developed along the way.

We prepared as best as we could for our holiday trips although we didn't know everything when we left, we gained knowledge as we travelled along. Most lessons are best learnt by application, experience and simply 'giving it a go'.

There are no mistakes, only opportunities.
- Tina Fey,
comedian

Perhaps you're concerned about something small like not being able to make it to all the board meetings? This can and does happen from time to time but technology these days enables members to communicate in a way we were once unable to do. There are many ways to manage meetings so don't let that hold you back.

Perhaps you're concerned because you don't know what boards are looking for and what's expected of you?

This is all part of the journey I'm going to take you on. Where to go, where to look, who to ask and what to ask, amongst other things. You will become more informed, overcome barriers, move forward and transform with confidence.

No matter where you're at in your board journey (with lots, little or no experience) you will get something out of this streamlined process.

You may be searching for greater meaning and purpose. Perhaps you want to advance your career or utilise skills you've developed? Or perhaps you simply want to contribute to better decision-making, make a difference or help others? Whatever the reason, this demystifying process will assist you to define and refine your thoughts, hopes and aspirations.

Have the confidence in yourself to realise that there are significant opportunities ahead of you. Getting on a board, using your skills, contributing to your heart's content, and positively making progress, is an exciting and an honourable achievement.

Wherever this moment leads you to, recognise its uniqueness. Your pathway to date and from here is yours and uniquely yours. It will be different (and potentially very different) to anyone else's. Your journey may take you where you expect, but more likely where you don't expect.

A new vision

My key takeaway for you from this chapter is the understanding and confidence of the opportunity. To help adopt a set of positive beliefs, write down some inspiring words or find inspiring images to help empower you and drive you into action.

Put them up on your wall to remind you on a daily basis. The aim is to sustain a positive frame of mind, giving you and your journey energy to reach beyond the horizon and fly high!

You're making some small but significant steps to kick off your new adventure! You're getting your mind into shape and ready to embrace what's ahead. Imagine your personal sense of fulfilment, happiness and satisfaction when you land that first interview.

More excitingly, imagine when you get that first offer of appointment. Even better, sitting in that seat for the first time at the board table. I remember when I did … I was stoked!

Believe in the opportunity. Believe in yourself.

Your new horizon is waiting …

Chapter 1 Checklist

- ☐ Opportunity
- ☐ Mindset
- ☐ Confidence
- ☐ On to Chapter 2

2

WHY FLY?

With your positive mindset and realisation of opportunity, the next important step in your journey is to fully understand what it is you're trying to find and where you're wanting to head.

What is your purpose for getting on a board? What are your reasons for wanting a seat at the board table?

You may have one reason, you may have many, and your reasons will differ from mine and the next person's. What's helpful is that you clarify and appreciate your own purpose/s so you can confirm your starting point and then your direction.

In the first chapter, we raised your knowledge and understanding about the world of boards and the opportunities available to you. In this second chapter, we're going to raise your awareness about you, yes, you!

We're going to acknowledge and pay attention to your hopes, dreams and aspirations. This chapter will help you define and refine your *Why?* and maybe even your *Why not?*

Your purpose

Appreciating your purpose and personal reasons gives greater focus. It helps to avoid getting down the track only to realise you're not where you thought you'd be or wanted to go, especially when you could have positioned yourself better in the beginning.

Landing in the wrong place can be disheartening and demoralising. Can you relate? Can you think of a time when you felt like this? Perhaps the circumstance may have been a misalignment between your personal values and the direction you went in? A clashing with your soul's desires?

Consider the message of author, motivational speaker and organisational consultant Simon Sinek. His message is simple – to firstly understand your drivers and defining your *why*. Simon advocates that if you can describe your *why*, then the *how* and the *what* follows (Sinek, 2009).

In his book *Start With Why*, Simon highlights how organisations often start with the 'What?' first. 'What is it we are selling?' and 'What service do we provide?' as opposed to 'Why do we sell this product or service?' Simon flips the thinking on its head with a philosophy we can equally apply to our personal lives.

Simon's message is driven by the suggestion that it's helpful to know the purpose of why you're doing something and to ensure there's alignment with your values. Hence, greater self-fulfilment and happiness.

With some listening to your heart but without overthinking, you will come to appreciate why you're seeking a board role. This insight into your own personal desires and drivers will give you clarity and direction for what's ahead. Importantly, this process feeds into helping you identify the most suitable destinations for you to fly to.

Further, you may also get a sense of what's over the horizon for you beyond a directorship and becoming a board member. Your board role could be a stepping stone to other exciting destinations. Be mindful though. This is a bonus but should not be your primary purpose or your *why* for getting on a board.

Whatever the reason or reasons, your board needs to be the right fit for you, and you for the board. Successful board positions are about matching the right people to the needs of the board, the organisation and its stakeholders. No one wants to waste their time, effort and energy, nor have a bad experience, especially first time around.

Boards are a collective of different but complementary skills. They exist for the purpose of making decisions on behalf of others, shaping and creating the future. Members work as part of a team, adding value in some form. Therefore, the alignment of personal drivers, purposes, beliefs and values is essential in order to gain personal fulfilment in achieving collective outcomes.

Non-executive director roles can be either voluntary or paid. Some positions are remunerated with directors' fees, while others offer reimbursement for expenses, and others have limited resources and are unable to offer financial compensation.

Best not to make assumptions, for example, that for-profit boards pay fees and not-for-profits don't pay fees. It is a case-by-case situation and fully depends on the individual organisation, just as pay does across other jobs, services or engagement contracts.

If your driver is for financial return, material benefit, a title or to push a separate agenda, you may need to reconsider boards as a career path. Boards don't exist for material returns, ego or the self-interested individual. This is a pretty important point and you may need to think twice if it's the perception of power which is attracting you!

Directors of boards also have what's referred to as a 'fiduciary duty'. This means individuals are legally obliged to act honestly, in good faith and on behalf of their organisation. They must put others' interests ahead of their own.

In discussing opportunities with aspiring directors, I have discovered varying reasons for people considering board work. Some want to make a meaningful contribution, others are seeking more effective outcomes, and others want to work with like-minded people. Some people are seeking something new, a change of focus, or a personal or career challenge.

I often hear expressions of the desire to contribute to social causes and wanting to make a difference to society. Sentiment is also often expressed about helping local charities or less fortunate communities overseas. For others, the prospect of board membership sparks a renewed interest in something they thought was previously unachievable without a long-lasting executive career.

Some of these people are professionals, both women and men, who have declined full-time employment to raise and care for their children. Many have found themselves embedded within their local communities, generating community support and building strong connections. These skills are becoming more recognised in the boardroom, adding value and enhancing board outcomes.

Assuming you're there for the right reasons and you do a fabulous job, a board or committee position may lead down various pathways, providing other short and long-term opportunities. Such a role may also broaden your network and raise your profile, potentially translating into future opportunities for careers, employment or business prospects.

Depending on your skills, capabilities and contributions, your board experience may evolve into a board career, as it did for me. Remember this is not your *why* but rather a secondary bonus resulting from doing the primary job well in the first place. As a non-executive director, you are first and foremost there to help direct and drive an organisation to positive and sustainable outcomes.

Why boards?

In recent years, there have been many – and significant – breaches of basic governance by organisations responsible for delivering health, wealth and financial services. Alongside corporate collapses, Australia has also seen a number of Royal Commissions (for example in banking, aged care and family violence), each investigating operational and governance failings of institutions. The findings of these reports highlight that poor corporate behaviours will no longer be tolerated.

One hopes that directors who set and maintain ethical board practices will be in greater demand. Combined with the capability and capacity in understanding contemporary and future trends, diligent directors will be well-positioned to make a positive difference for the boards of tomorrow.

This is not just understanding but applying a holistic approach to decision-making across the many facets of society. Considerations include community needs, environmental conservation, infrastructure conditions and economic health, as well as increasing the integration of sustainability, governance, risk and ethics. Some of this seems to have been (and perhaps still is) missing from the thought processes at the highest levels, including those from some of the largest and supposedly most trusted corporations and organisations.

'What on earth is governance?' you ask? Some know it and practise it. Some know it and don't practise it! Others have vaguely heard of it and others have no idea. Governance might sound a bit daunting but it's actually easy to comprehend and instil, and not to be feared.

Governance is the glue which helps organisations run effectively and efficiently. It is one of direction and oversight, forming a very important part of an entity's ongoing viability and success. Governance is the framework of elements by which an organisation, business, community group, and even a project, is controlled. It relates to the legal obligations, structures, systems and policies in place that hold it together.

Careful, this isn't to be confused with the concept of management, which refers to doing the work (as in the implementation of decisions and delivery of operations).

You might agree with me when I say that governance is one of the most unsexy words you've ever heard of – am I right? A topic often perceived as boring, demanding and distracting from being able to get the 'real' job done. This is probably because the concept resembles a tedious set of rules, instructions, systems and documentation aimed at making sure things are done right – properly, legally and morally.

There are many definitions of governance, but I like this simple description by the Governance Institute of Australia (GIA), which particularly notes the key elements, integration and accountability across the board and its organisation. 'Governance encompasses the system by which an organisation is controlled and operates, and the mechanisms by which it, and its people, are held to account. Ethics, risk management, compliance and administration are all elements of governance' (GIA, 2019).

When governance is done well, it is known as 'good governance'. Good governance is like a well-oiled machine where everything is integrated and all moving parts work together.

When governance is done exceptionally well, it can be referred to as 'great governance'. I like this term as it highlights a diligent and proactive approach which goes over and above standard expectations. Irrespective, the level of governance can be the difference between success and failure, and it's the responsibility of the board to make sure it's done well.

When governance is not done well, it can be fatal for the organisation. Sadly, we've all seen examples of poor corporate governance and practices – some incredible case-in-points of directors, executives and officers who don't appear to be there for the right reasons and who are not doing their job properly.

Governance might seem dry and mundane, but there's not much joy in seeing your personal finances or superannuation held by an organisation with a board and its directors who don't demonstrate good, if not great, governance!

In response to these poor behaviours, emerging issues and growing community expectations, the ASX recently reviewed and updated their Corporate Governance Principles and Recommendations. These are eight key principles for listed companies to consider, effective 1 January 2020 (ASX Corporate Governance Council, 2019).

The eight key principles are:

- Lay solid foundations for management and oversight
- Structure the board to be effective and add value
- Instil a culture of acting lawfully, ethically and responsibly
- Safeguard the integrity of corporate reports
- Make timely and balanced disclosure
- Respect the rights of security holders
- Recognise and manage risk
- Remunerate fairly and responsibly

These principles are not mandatory for ASX-listed entities but are rather suggested practices to meet the expectations of shareholders. Likewise, they do provide a benchmark for non-ASX organisations and entities to aspire to.

One might suggest that good governance and other good practices are 'common sense'. I find the reference to common sense fascinating. Many years ago, a friend once said, 'How can there be common sense when everyone is different, with an individual perspective?'

I reflected on this and it may be helpful for you too, given 'common sense' is such as well-used term. Think about it … realistically why would everyone necessarily have the same understanding, standards and expectations? Why would we have commonality of our thoughts, when our lives, experiences, interpretations, perceptions and values are so varied? There's difficulty assuming that 'common sense' exists.

Key questions

When people learn about my numerous board roles or directorships, they often say, 'I want to get on a board!' or they ask, 'How did you get on a board?', 'What's it like to be on a board?' and 'What do I need to do to get on a board?'

These questions have been asked of me by people from many different backgrounds and levels of experience, including experienced executives and entrepreneurs. I find this curiosity a reflection of people in various states of board-awareness, understanding and interest, irrespective of their role in society.

This constant posing and answering of these questions are what inspired me and gave me purpose to write this book. Helping you and helping others like you, as aspiring, emerging or experienced board members, is a privilege. It is my pleasure to guide and equip you with the tools you need to achieve your goal.

In further considering my *why* and purpose for this book, although not a prolific reader as a child, I really enjoyed learning and writing. As a teen learning about goal setting, I was encouraged to write down some future goals. To my amazement, I had an undeniable urge and scribbled 'Write a book'. I didn't know what it would be about but just always thought that I'd love to write a book one day.

Despite my overwhelming urge to write, I didn't think it would ever really happen, given my lack of confidence, lack of skills and lack of topic at that point. The penny dropped one day when I considered how I could answer all the questions being asked of me about boards.

With so much to share, I realised a book would be the best way for me to put down and compile so many of my thoughts. A concise way to present and share the information. A sort of manual outlining a blueprint to help others navigate their own flying journey to the boardroom.

Suddenly, there was my *why* – my *why* for that book I was going to write one day. This gave me the clarity, direction and drive to write over 40,000 words!

I also realised my bigger, broader *why*. This was an expression of my love of imparting knowledge, sharing information, teaching and empowering others. To enable you to have the tools and learn how to use them yourself. It was also at this time that I reconnected with the enjoyment I received out of coaching springboard diving back in my university days – the satisfaction of helping others and seeing them achieve their goals.

I'm going to be bold and blow my own trumpet about this book by saying 'I'm proud of myself!' These are a few words I'd like for you to teach yourself to say. Here's a little tip for you: make sure you celebrate your achievements, if not with others, then at least with yourself.

Find a format that works for you and give yourself recognition, fulfilment and reward for your efforts. So often, we don't share or acknowledge our achievements but what a great excuse for some fun!

My *why*

I'd like to share more of my story with you. It highlights many of the key points I would like for you to take away from this book. This background will also give you an understanding of me, who I am and what makes me tick, as well as giving you insights from my experiences.

Once upon a time if you asked me, 'Why boards?' I wouldn't have been able to articulate the answer. I had a feeling, an urge I had to follow. I had a lot to contribute and felt I could add value as a result of my skills, insight and experience. I felt I could make a difference in setting directions, making decisions and determining final outcomes.

If I reflect far enough into my history, I can see a common theme. Even in my early days of high school, I ended up being the class representative for the Student Representative Council (SRC). Not just once but twice! If my memory serves me well, in one case it was more a matter that no one else had put their hand up and I became the lucky winner! Later in Year 12, I was elected into a leadership role so I like to think I had something to offer!

The notion of making decisions, developing future strategies and instilling great governance instinctively appealed to me. Many would say I was mad, but I was always interested in business as well as sustainability, where the health of our communities and environment were not compromised but otherwise preserved or enhanced.

To me, business and sustainability has always gone hand-in-hand, mutually inclusive rather than exclusively related. I even used to skip my engineering lectures to go to the lunchtime lectures at the ASX to get my dose of business studies.

The type of work boards do fascinated me. My husband recalls a conversation we had in our early twenties where I said I wanted to work on boards or with boards. I don't remember the discussion and I was blown away when he told me only once I was halfway through writing this book!

I recall early on thinking that it would be awesome to be on a board … one day. One day when I'm retired with grey hair, great wisdom and time to be able to commit to such a role. At that stage, I hadn't considered joining a board because in my mind they were reserved for the older, the experienced and the executive. Yet I held the goal for some later stage in life, as I perceived it not to be a possibility for a youngster in the short-term.

How funny to reflect and see the path I've travelled. Less than ten years later, I had reached a point in my career where I was bored, really bored! I needed something more meaningful, a challenge and change of focus.

I yearned for something that would allow me to express more of who I was, both personally as well as professionally. I needed to exercise my range of skills and work on projects that would make a difference with positive outcomes. I expressed to my mentor that I'd considered doing a Master of Business Administration (MBA) but the commitment seemed overwhelming given I was embarking on having a family.

During our conversation, my mentor asked, 'Have you heard of the Company Directors Course?' As he explained and described the program to me, the fire in my belly came alive.

Within six months of that conversation with my mentor, I completed the face-to-face course. I loved every moment of the program, sinking my teeth into business studies and meeting other like-minds and those with similar interests.

I learnt more about corporate strategic planning, risk management, governance and financial management. Having worked in the public and private sectors, I found it interesting to compare the differences between boards and committees in both sectors.

Around the time I finished the coursework, I had fallen pregnant with my first child. Some months later at the graduation ceremony, I was very obviously pregnant! In fact, about 8.5 months along and struggling to move.

To see me in the room must have been amusing. I was one of the few ladies who had completed the course, a youngster in the crowd, just off thirty years old and certainly the only one under five foot! Not only that, I had a big bun in the oven. Not quite the fitting image of a traditional board member in the mid-2000s!

In my mind, it was only too normal to be there receiving recognition for something I graduated from. I had put my mind into this program and completed the course, irrespective of my gender, age, height, background, qualifications, etc. I saw no barriers and made no issues. I just focused on the direction I was heading in.

Before I had finished the coursework of the program, I had seen an advertisement seeking nominations for board vacancies. The organisation promoting the board role was a peak industry, networking and training organisation for local government employees.

I instinctively felt my younger perspective and connection to the next generation could help enhance the service and products on offer. I felt I could generate more valued outcomes for the sector.

When I first saw this role, I didn't think much about it, because the story I was telling myself was that it was too soon. I'd only just finished the course. Yet there was a gut feeling, saying, *That'd be cool. Reckon I could do that!* Meanwhile the logic and fear in my head said, 'There's no way you'll get appointed!' Fortunately, this feeling in my stomach was far stronger and led me to give it a go.

Given the organisation was member-based, it was a case of throwing my hat in the ring for the election process. I filled out a nomination form complete with the endorsement and support of two colleagues (a requirement of the process).

The nominations didn't go to vote. The number of candidates equalled the number of vacancies and by way of a lucky strike, I was appointed to the board! My first board role! I'd been appointed as a non-executive director to a peak industry board. There I was, in the boardroom sitting amongst CEOs and senior executives from the industry. It was very daunting but very exciting at the same time!

I was just off thirty, hadn't climbed the corporate ladder and wasn't a CEO or C-suite officer (chief-level manager). Despite my luck, what I could offer was a younger perspective to support workers in local government with their roles. To help them deliver services to enhance urban development and infrastructure, protect natural assets, enrich social and community services, and help local business growth. My *why* for applying was to help equip others with the capability to make better decisions and take better actions to create a better tomorrow.

I was fairly happy with my efforts! I had stepped right out of my comfort zone, put up the challenge and achieved my goal. Most importantly, I had gone in with good intentions, followed my heart and intuition, and put in the necessary work.

With a new qualification from the course and a baby on the way, I was no longer bored. I was on a board! Not long after having commenced this new journey, I was now clearly heading in a new direction and flying to a new destination after having landed my first directorship.

With a taste for board work, it wasn't long before I threw my hat in the ring again and again, to what became a rolling sequence of positions and subsequently, a default board career. My hopes had been to get on one board one day, but to be sitting on multiple boards was quite unexpected.

Fly forward over fifteen years and I've had ten appointments on eight different boards and committees across a range of industries and sectors, including five paid positions. These roles were responsible for alpine and ski resorts, coastline planning and management, township infrastructure and development, professional development, tertiary education and early childhood education.

What a privilege! In all, my appointments have accumulated to an equivalent of over eighteen years of service on boards and committees. This time doesn't include other working committees and judging panels which I've also participated on for various projects. I couldn't have predicted it and wouldn't have believed you if you would have told me this when I first ventured along this path.

For each of my board positions, there was a different *why*, a different reason depending on the purpose of the organisation and the type of board. My personal reasonings evolved around the conservation of natural environments, effective utilisation of infrastructure, enhancement of social and community capability, and the optimisation of financial resources.

I utilised and applied my skills where I could. I drew on my expertise in engineering, environmental management, community development, economic development, risk management, governance and strategic planning. I drew on my skills in analytical thinking, problem-solving and creative solutions. All to reduce impacts, drive greater benefits and increase valued outputs.

Some of the differences I've personally made at board level to date have included, but not limited to:

- Clarifying the vision and strategic directions of entities
- Developing realistic strategic plans, priorities and timeframes
- Improving risk policies and procedures
- Refining board and organisational policies and practices
- Scrutinising budgets, financial plans and value of expenditure
- Assessing the social, environmental and financial impacts of decisions
- Determining the merit of property and infrastructure proposals
- Highlighting engineering and asset considerations for future cost implications
- Assessing product options to boost organisational viability
- Highlighting potential changes to legislation for better outcomes
- Enhancing community and stakeholder communications and relationships.

Board work has enabled me to draw on my strengths at the highest levels for organisations, businesses and community groups. I have appreciated the chance to be challenged and gain a good dose of mental stimulation, especially given my other key job was primarily caring for two young children.

I receive and continue to receive fulfilment from seeing things done better. This is a big *why* for me. So much so that now I help boards, directors, executives and those aspiring to boards to fulfil their potential and better position themselves for the next phase and over the horizon. I love seeing other people achieve, whether for business viability, a better community, a healthier environment or another enriching goal.

Enough about me, let's focus on you! Imagine if you had taken this journey of mine? How would you feel?

I'd like to demystify the process for you and help guide you to fulfil your purpose, live your dream and experience the same satisfaction.

Your *why*

So why is it that you wish to take this journey? What are your reasons? Are you seeking a new challenge, social change, greater productivity or just want to contribute to making things better? Or are you perhaps lacking interest or meaning in your current life direction?

Your drivers may be conscious or subconscious, but it's important to tease them out to appreciate what you want to achieve and why. Do you intuitively know your purpose? You want to connect with the inner you!

Let's free your mind and understand your *why*. This process is designed for you to clarify and appreciate your personal desires, drivers and motivations to be on a board; your true purpose for embarking on this new adventure. There's no need for it to be extensive, but sufficient enough to help you gain clarity so that you can articulate your message to someone else. 'Why?' is likely to be one of the first questions you will be asked when applying for a board role.

In working through this process to gain an indication of your *why*, you'll want to explore some simple questions like:

- What's important to me?
- What's important to my family and community?
- Where do I want to focus my energies?
- What difference do I want to make?
- Who do I want to help?

This is just a snapshot to grasp your personal objectives and purpose. Be true to you. If you're uncertain, perhaps come back to this step after a few chapters. Most importantly, don't get caught up in paralysis by analysis where thinking overtakes your ability to act. Just start to progress through this process. Remember that, in many ways, this is part of your life journey and your *why* may develop and refine over time.

Whilst you can possibly and very easily overthink, try not to. The key is asking the right questions to get the right answers. If you're feeling overwhelmed, recognise your intuition and pay respect to what feels right.

Most importantly, stay connected to your gut feelings. Simon Sinek goes on to further explain that this gut feeling or intuition stems from the limbic part of our brain which is connected to our emotions (Sinek, 2009). Hence, the reason why we can feel at ease in placing trust in our gut instinct.

Many successful entrepreneurs have also stated that their greatest success has been when they listened to their intuition (Wilson, 2018). If you're like me, you'll find comfort in this.

Reasoning

Whatever your pathway, it's important to know that what you put into this journey, you will get out. Like anything, this can be a pivotal point of enlightenment. As you travel along your journey, whether it be personal, professional or about boards, be sure to check in on your *why* on a regular basis. You'll find greatest fulfilment along a path that fits your purpose, your values and what's important to you, your family, your community and the world around you.

Equipped with a level of board-consciousness and appreciation of your personal desires and drivers, I hope you're beginning to build a foundation to stand on which is strongly supported by a positive state of mind.

In the next chapters, we will further explore and demystify the world of boards and committees. This information will provide you with some essential knowledge, understanding about destinations to fly to and the preparations you'll need to take-off on your flight.

Whilst we've been asking *why?* I equally challenge you with *why not?* Why not fly and why not be true to you?

Live your beliefs and you can turn the world around
- Henry David Thoreau,
philosopher, poet and writer

Chapter 2 Checklist

- ☐ Governance
- ☐ Questions
- ☐ Why?
- ☐ On to Chapter 3

3

DESTINATIONS

A common question I'm asked is, 'What board should I aim for?' Not unlike travel destinations, how do you know where to go if you don't know what's out there?

I'm pleased to suggest that it's time for some 'board-appreciation'! Not unlike the concept of wine-appreciation or beer-appreciation, you get to explore the concept of boards, get to know some of the finer details and get an understanding of the different types of boards.

I'd like to educate you and give you context around the world of boards so that by the end of this chapter, you'll be equipped with a this greater level of knowledge and a deeper understanding of the type of boards and opportunities that are available to you.

You'll also gain an appreciation for what boards do, what they're governed by, how they're set up, how they're appointed, who sits on them and how they work. The benefit is that you will feel a sense of relief with many 'Ah-ha' and 'Now I get it!' moments.

Board basics

Boards exist for both large and small entities, and across all industries and sectors.

Groups of individuals such as these collectively oversee the activities of an entity. Irrespective of the nature and type, they are required to function effectively, to guide and govern the organisation.

Boards are responsible for delivering sustainable outcomes and value for both the short and long-term. The group makes decisions, sets directions and strategies, and ensures that all frameworks, policies, procedures and systems are in place to effectively operate the business. It has the responsibility to ensure that the operational team can deliver the strategic outcomes and monitors progress toward these goals.

The world of boards and working on a board is a very different dynamic to what some may be used to. Given the board is a high level decision-making unit, board activities can be contrasting to managerial or operational duties. The role of a non-executive director is one of oversight and decision-making as opposed to that of an executive director who is responsible for the operational work.

For some, moving into a non-executive role and commencing board work can take a bit of getting used to. Some can find it difficult to sit on the sidelines calling the shots rather than being in there managing the operations; hence doing the decision-making but not the implementation.

Important to note, there is no one-size board that fits all organisations. It is a case-by-case situation where a board's role depends on the needs of the organisation at any given point in time.

The purpose of a board can vary. It is governed by the business model and what stage the business or organisation is in.

Have you heard of a 'business lifecycle'? This is not dissimilar to the life journey of us as humans. In a nutshell, this is the journey of a business, organisation or entity over time.

Business stages generally comprise a beginning, through a growth phase to become established, mature or expand and then, if declining, reinvent themselves or come to an end. These transitions of a business might look like what is shown in Figure 2.

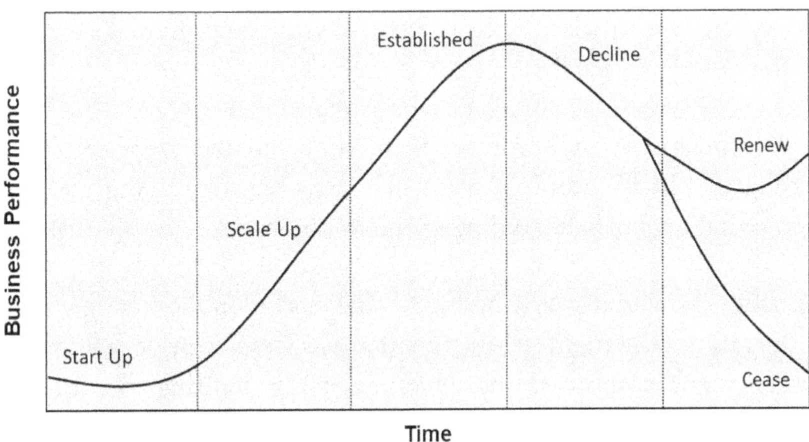

Figure 2: The business lifecycle

There are many graphs out there displaying variations of the business lifecycle. While the stages and language can change, they essentially highlight the same process.

The key point is that conducting business is a dynamic artform and there is a constant need for review and decision-making. Think of an organisation you're involved with – where does it sit in the cycle?

Each phase of a business lifecycle presents a different focus and set of challenges (Chen, 2014). The needs, skill sets and skill mixes required in each stage to effectively steer the organisation relies heavily on specific and specialist input, insight and expertise.

The board of an organisation in start-up phase is very different to one which has reached maturity, and likewise for each of the stages. Therefore, the composition of the board, its size and shape at any point in time, is best informed by the organisation's position in its lifecycle.

Think about your personal journey throughout different life stages. What have been your different needs? Did you get the right advice, from the right people, at the right time? Organisations too have different needs in order to transition properly and stay on track. Hence the reason why the right people with the right skills serving on the board at a particular time is crucial.

Not all businesses will operate throughout all the lifecycle phases highlighted in Figure 2. Many will cease operating along the way, even dying an early death during the initial stages.

Statistics show that nearly half of businesses fail in the first few years of operation. The main reasons cited are as a result of poor strategic management, cash flows and governance, highlighting the need for effective oversight and a suitable mix of skills (Price, 2017).

Sadly, this stuff isn't rocket science! And this isn't limited to small business but also large corporations, private family businesses, public authorities and community organisations who have and can suffer the same fate.

As a non-executive director, understanding where you and your skills best fit within the business lifecycle is valuable. What's even more valuable is having the insight and strength to know when your best work has been made.

A good board member will acknowledge when their contributions have optimised an organisation. If their skills are limited or no longer relevant to what's needed at the time, they will step down or offer to remove themselves from the board.

On the flip side, others can suffer from egotistical issues – an ego which can take over, dampen progress, and be detrimental to both the board and the business. Can you think of an example?

Types of boards

There are different types of boards, depending on the legal business structure, nature of the organisation and their purpose for existing.

To keep it simple, boards and committees can be generally categorised into three functional types: governing, operational and advisory. Each having their own specific accountabilities and characteristics.

To better provide an outline of each, Table 1 below describes the functional board types.

Functional Board Types	Description
Governing	The board has legal responsibilities and provides governing and strategic oversight, direction and decision-making only. Implementation and operations are undertaken by appointed staff. For example, the board of an ASX company or a public authority.
Operational	The board may or may not have legal responsibility but has dual carriage as a working board, responsible for both decision-making and implementation for the organisation. For example, a small not-for-profit organisation or a local community group.
Advisory	The board has no legal responsibility but provides expert insight for decision-making consideration. It is responsible for providing independent advice only; no decision-making or implementation. For example, a panel of experts reporting to a governing board.

Table 1: Functional board types

When initially in start-up mode, or if the organisation doesn't have sufficient funds, an operational board may be put in place. Board members will undertake both the decision-making and legwork until the business reaches a point in its journey where a strategic board can be appointed.

Alternatively, an advisory board may be appointed without financial accountability and provide independent expert advice and guidance to the governing board.

Boards have a distinct role and responsibility for directing an organisation's activities. However, their purpose is driven by their business structure, the type of organisation they are and what phase they are in.

In a nutshell, but not strictly, organisations are commercially-focused or community-focused, falling into one of four types as shown in Figure 3 and Table 2.

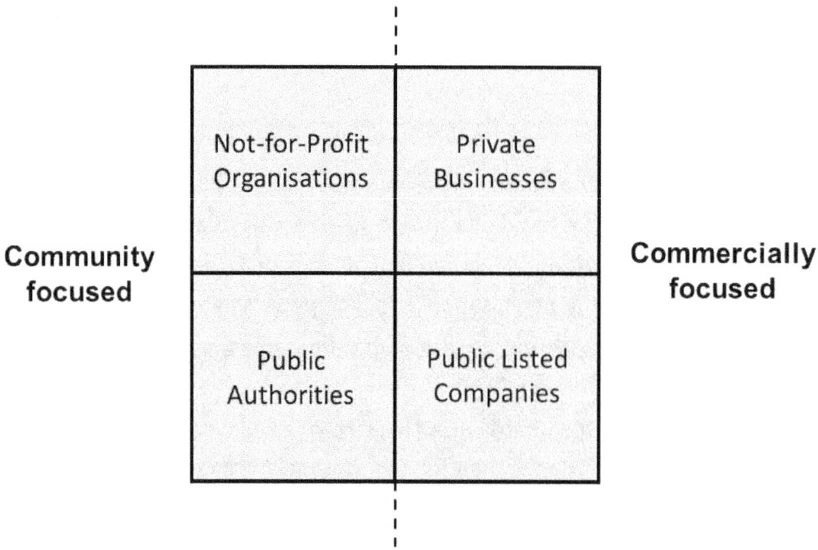

Figure 3: Types of organisations

Organisation Type	Description
Not-for-Profit Organisation	Non-government social and community entities established for a specific purpose with profits re-invested to help humanity and/or the environment.
Public Authority	Locally small to nationally large government organisations and authorities delivering public services and community benefits.
Private Business	Privately owned, small businesses to large international companies, generally aimed at generating profits.
Public Listed Company	Medium to large organisations, aimed at generating profits which are available on the stock exchange for public trading.

Table 2: Description of organisations

What examples come to mind for each of these categories? A family business is often privately owned, major banks are often publicly listed on the stock exchange, hospitals can be public service providers, and sports clubs and charities often operate as not-for-profit enterprises.

Understanding the types, characteristics and duties of different entities should provide you with greater insight and sense for which type of boards you may be most aligned to. Irrespective of the type, they all fit a business structure, must be viable and have sufficient support to operate effectively.

Board responsibilities

Regardless of the type of board, the responsibilities are not dissimilar. Whether the board is overseeing a small community organisation, start-up social enterprise, government organisation or a large multinational corporation, boards and directors effectively have the same duties and must act diligently.

Boards are responsible for administering the organisation or entity on behalf of stakeholders, including shareholders, investors, ratepayers or members.

Board members collectively have carriage for setting the short and long-term direction, and making important decisions about vision, strategy, policy, risks and finances.

Boards are established and enacted as a result of legislation or imposed directions. These regulations, constitutions, instruments of appointment or business requirements inform and give rise to how the entity is to be established and governed. The geographical location of organisations or their jurisdiction of registration can dictate how a board and its business must be governed.

The set of principles explaining a board's governance and conduct is outlined in a key document known as the board's 'charter'. This is an overarching set of details containing and outlining information relating to the board, such as roles, responsibilities, purpose, objectives, positions, member appointments and terms of appointment.

One of the key roles of the board is to appoint an Executive Officer or Chief Executive Officer (CEO) to implement decisions and directives as determined by the board. The CEO subsequently allocates suitable resources to deliver the organisation's operations such as the appointment of a management team and staff.

A good board will regularly review the performance of its CEO and organisation. This is to ensure all levels and all efforts are heading together in the direction set by the board.

Board composition

Another important aspect of good governance is the composition of boards. Like our bodies, boards come in all shapes and sizes, and there is no one-size-fits-all. They may comprise business owners, representatives, shareholders, stakeholders or independent members.

The makeup of a board is based on the purpose, direction and phase of the organisation. The breadth of skills necessary for boards are compiled into what's called a 'skills matrix'. This dictates what boards look for in their membership (which we will explore further in the next chapter).

There is greater recognition these days about the impact that skill mix and board membership have on the overall effectiveness of organisations. Harvard Law School highlights board composition as a key global trend (Goodman, Martin, & O'Kelley, 2018).

Boards have a chairperson and sometimes (but not always) there is a deputy chairperson. The chair, the head of the board, is charged with co-ordinating the board and board meetings.

Depending on the type of organisation, chairs may be referred to using different terminology. These include president (and vice president) of not-for-profit and incorporated organisations, mayor (and deputy mayor) in the case of councils and local government, and convenor, for example as another for committees. Sometimes these terms are used interchangeably by many but do relate to specific sectors or types of organisations.

Many boards also appoint subcommittees. They are established to make best use of members' time and expertise. These are smaller groups made up of board members, delegated or charged with specific roles and responsibilities, on behalf of the whole board. Particular issues requiring a deeper level of investigation or consideration can be tackled by those with expert skills without consuming valuable board meeting time of all board members.

The establishment of subcommittees depends on the needs, requirements and desires of the board. Sometimes a subcommittee may involve external members to provide additional independent expert or specialist advice to enhance the strength of the committee.

Subcommittees may be continuous for a full board term, short-term or for a particular timeframe. They may be initiated for activities like events or special projects with a defined start and end date. For smaller boards, these committees may be hands-on, with board members undertaking some of the tasks themselves.

Do you know of any board subcommittees? Some examples include, but are certainly not limited to, focusing on finance, risk, ethics, strategy, sustainability and communications subcommittees.

In my time as a non-executive director, I've been involved with and sat on numerous subcommittees dealing with a wide range of matters. These have included:

- Remuneration committee, responsible for reviewing the CEO's annual performance.
- Strategic planning committees, responsible for driving long-term plans, assessing development plans and preparing masterplans.
- Planning and infrastructure committee, charged with assessing major infrastructure and investment plans.
- Communications committee, responsible for implementing effective messaging.
- Awards committees, charged with overseeing the delivery of a major conference event and industry award judging.
- Event committee, responsible for delivering a major local community open day.

Each subcommittee role drew upon my key skills but also provided me with further invaluable experience about boards, judgements and decisions.

Board appointments

You may have come to realise by now that there is so much that varies with boards and committees. The process for appointing board members is no different and again depends on the founding nature, enacting constitution or legal and policy frameworks surrounding the board.

Appointments can be made by various means. These include via nomination, application and voting processes, by members of an organisation, parliament, shareholders, stakeholders, or by the chairperson and the board itself.

Just to add to the mix, the terms of appointment can also differ. Sometimes lengths of initial appointments may be for a year only, perhaps two or three years or longer, and may commence at the start of a year, on a certain date such as an AGM, or the anniversary of a set date.

Each board, their strategic direction and stage of operation, will dictate what skill mix is required to help propel the organisation forward. This will also inform what reappointments or new appointments are made.

Think of the different boards that you know of? Perhaps an organisation you've worked for or you're involved with? Maybe a company on the ASX you have shares in, a school committee, local sporting group, council or authority, family business or perhaps your own business?

These are all very different entities, each requiring a sound group of skilled personnel to oversee its organisation and make decisions for the efficient and effective delivery of products or services. Think about the size and shape of the board. How many members sit on the board? What skills do they have? How long are they appointed for?

Board clarity

If you become overwhelmed or concerned that you don't understand, don't be hard on yourself. It's a learning process and it just means you're not quite there … yet. Let it sink in, as you're beginning a new journey. You're not expected to know everything immediately and you don't have to remember everything now. This is an introduction, to give you an overview and a greater sense of what boards are all about.

I hope this chapter has provided you with greater insight – greater clarity of the purpose of boards, their role, the type of boards there are, how they're different and why they're different.

I also hope you've gained a deeper appreciation of some of the terminology used to describe boards and directors, aspects of boards and structures of boards. I trust what has become clearer to you are the potential destinations ahead for your board journey.

Given your awareness of this whole new world and the places out there, the next stage is to understand which board/s you should steer towards. To keep the ball rolling, I'd like to now take you through a phase focused on understanding the skills needed for different boards. This will be key in helping you save time and effort whilst you find the right board for your unique package of skills and strengths.

Ready? Let's go and find the paths and flights which best suit you.

The great aim of education is not knowledge but action.
– Herbert Spencer,
philosopher and sociologist

Chapter 3 Checklist

- ☐ Purpose of a board
- ☐ Board structures
- ☐ Board appointments
- ☐ On to Chapter 4

4

FLIGHT PATH

Imagine a place where you can totally be yourself. A circumstance where you can tap into and draw on all you've got: your talents, your skills, and your educated and insightful views, to share what's in your heart.

Jack Delosa, a young Australian entrepreneur, author, founder and CEO of The Entourage, is living proof of following your heart, being authentic and drawing on all that makes you an individual.

In Jack's books *Unwritten* and *Unprofessional* he provides insights about untraditional approaches to work and life and making the world a better place. Jack cracked the mould by turning his back on what is deemed a 'normal' career development pathway as a business owner and professional.

In his journey, Jack has remained true to himself. He took his skill set, learnings and future insights and combined them with a personal life objective to make a difference in the world. He calls it 'living a life for purpose', where doing good and profits don't have to be mutually exclusive.

*Inventing a better tomorrow begins with
acknowledging that the future does not need to
resemble the past.*
- Jack Delosa,
founder and CEO

We have an amazing world and it is what we do with it that matters! To be part of a board charged with the responsibility to contribute to future decision-making is a privilege.

Sometimes though, grasping how to get there can be a challenge. So that you're not left in the dark, I'm keen to help you with this. I'd like to help you identify what boards are looking for and what your best pathway options are for your board journey and beyond.

In this chapter, we will explore some of the essential skills needed to effectively get onto a board and contribute to the future you want. That way you can better plan your journey to get yourself that seat at the board table and make the difference you want.

As already highlighted, the composition of a board is a reflection of the type of organisation it is and the purpose of the particular board. With this mind, I want to share something exciting with you in this chapter to make it much easier for you to appreciate your best board fit, options and pathways. This tool will help set you in the right direction and further enable you to move forward with confidence.

Essential board skills

When looking for a board role, it's a matter of knowing what boards are seeking. There are some specific fundamental prerequisites for any board, but depending on the type of board, there can be other criteria to consider. Depending on the alignment with your strengths, this knowledge will inform what flight paths are best available to you.

There are many myths and ill-informed perceptions out there about boards. Whilst many high-profile corporate boards draw on executive experience for a high degree of expertise, knowledge and skill, there are many other boards that do not require the same degree or level of experience.

A multinational listed company requires a significant combination of attributes and experience in their line of business, industry or sector. Whereas a smaller local organisation functions and makes effective decisions using a different set of skills, knowledge and experience. In either case, boards are looking for people with relevant skills to create a complimentary and competent mix of capabilities and capacities to successfully steer their organisation.

A reminder for you: the future doesn't always have to reflect the past! With increasing community, stakeholder and shareholder expectations, there is a growing need and desire for the right people, with the right skills, for both the short-term and long-term.

No matter the direction, objectives or status of an organisation, a suitable and appropriate skill mix present on the board is essential. Some organisations are still learning that without the breadth of appropriate expertise and insight amongst their decision-making group, progress is difficult and future operations can be compromised.

A broad skill set and experience base on the board adds significant value. It helps improve the board's decision-making process, innovation, performance and sustainability of the organisation (Koumouli, 2018). This is a difficult point to argue against when the skills and attributes reflect the needs and desires of the community, client, customer, consumer or stakeholder. Hence, a reminder of why greater diversity is being sought by many boards, to ensure there are reasonable and responsible viewpoints.

As a newbie to the world of boards, take comfort in knowing that you don't have to know everything in intricate detail. You and all your fellow board members aren't expected to each have all the necessary knowledge and skills applicable individually, but rather to ensure that they exist collectively amongst the group.

You are however, as enshrined within legislation, expected to behave in good faith and undertake the role with due care and the diligence of a reasonable person, in the best interest of the organisation and for the right purpose (Australian Government, 2001).

As a non-executive director and board member, you're expected to raise issues, ask questions and explore matters. It is also your role to seek advice and clarity, and determine the actions to be undertaken.

As a minimum, it is important for non-executive directors to have an understanding of strategy, risk, governance, ethics and finance. Without these board basics, you could be limiting your opportunities. I also like to include sustainability in this list too.

Financial skills are the one essential ingredient for every non-executive director, no matter how passionate or technically minded you may be. Irrespective of the field, sector or industry, the reality is that every organisation needs to pay sufficient attention to the accounts and balance sheet for its survival.

A social enterprise dedicated to assisting the neediest of people will not sustain itself into the future, deliver its vision, and provide the help if the board is not able to effectively understand the business model and manage its finances.

Appropriate and adequate resource management underpins quality service and product delivery and gives greater assurance in achieving the entity's purpose.

You're not expected to be an accountant, but financial literacy is probably one of the easiest things to learn. Do some research, training or ask an expert. The more questions you ask, the more informed you become. As a minimum, organisations and businesses (irrespective of size) require core skills amongst their board members.

When I talk about core skills, I'm really talking about four particular types of skills and attributes being sought. This is how I like to describe, define and package up essential board skills, as highlighted in Figure 4. A good combination of these will increase your chances of taking flight.

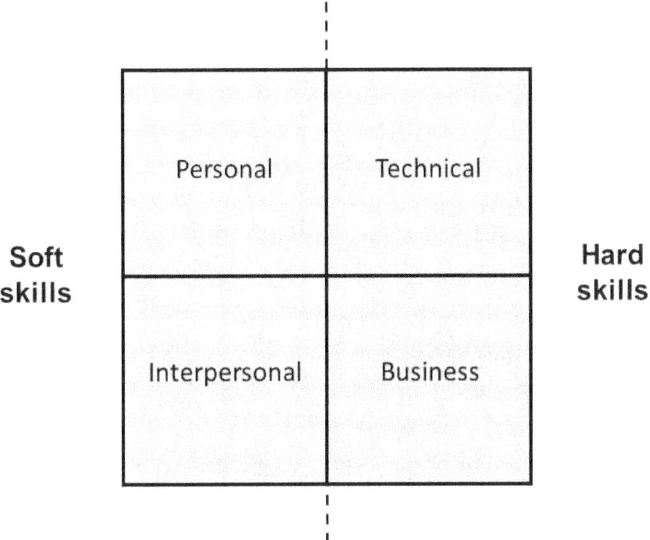

Figure 4: Board skills

'Hard skills' include essential technical and business expertise. This relates to your knowledge or specialist experience in a particular field, industry or sector, and your skills in business administration. These competencies may have developed from professional practice, volunteer experience or specific personal life experiences.

Complementing these hard skills are a range of 'soft skills'. These are your human skills. Those personal attributes and qualities which you draw upon and apply to your relationships with others and interactions with the world around you.

These soft skills are essential ingredients such as listening and communicating, and qualities such as respect, trust, transparency, appreciation, and a good moral and ethical compass. Equally, good doses of commitment and emotional intelligence will also play an integral part in both your individual and collective board success.

Ideally, these skills have provided you with the foundation upon which you have built your hard skills.

Boards seek different attributes at different times when looking for new members. The type of board, roles and responsibilities will dictate what boards are seeking. Criteria will depend on the existing composition, direction of the organisation and point in the organisation's lifecycle.

Future skills

Demand for the range in crucial hard and soft skills is likely to continue. Organisations like the World Economic Forum (WE Forum) and other futuristic commentators highlight the importance of lifelong learning, and key 21st century skills to best equip us and keep us relevant in the future.

The WE Forum is often quoted regarding future skills. Each year, they produce 'The Future of Jobs Report' which is an international snapshot of economic changes and development. The report outlines trends, strategies and skills across industries, regions and workforces to ensure we can adapt to the multitude and speed of changes ahead.

According to WE Forum (World Economic Forum, 2018), the top ten future projected skills for 2022 are:

- Analytical thinking and innovation
- Active learning and learning strategies
- Creativity, originality and initiative
- Technology design and programming
- Critical thinking and analysis
- Complex problem-solving
- Leadership and social influence
- Emotional intelligence
- Reasoning, problem-solving and ideation
- Systems analysis and evaluation.

Interestingly, the majority of these skills are soft skills. One could only expect these are a minimum for anyone considering a non-executive role with any type or size of organisation.

Given we are significantly submerged in the technology era, I like the notion of digital competency which is referred to as the Digital Quotient (DQ) (Cocorocchia, 2018).

Much like the Intellectual Quotient (IQ) is a measure of general understanding, DQ relates to our ability to use and apply digital technology responsibly, creatively and innovatively to develop solutions and solve problems.

Our world is dictated by many apps, platforms and programs, as well as networks, mobile communications and social media. This isn't always well understood by non-executive directors and board members, particularly those who haven't kept up with rapid changes in technology.

Such advances need to be understood to fully appreciate the impact on and benefits to operations. This is an acknowledgement of the contemporary business landscape looking forward into the future rather than backward into the past.

Having said all that, a well-balanced cross section of skills and perspectives provides a breeding ground for healthy decision-making. This involves a good mix of skills and attributes combined with a range of ages, abilities, cultures and backgrounds working together to create outcomes for now and into the future.

Not only may a complementary mix of skills improve decision-making, but it may also develop the board capabilities of its members. The more individuals with sound board experience, the greater the pool of suitable candidates that communities and corporations can draw upon for other key roles and leadership positions in society.

Board pathways

To understand suitability and pathways to boardrooms, there are some basic alignments which give prospective members a head start. This is a no-brainer, but support of the fundamental philosophy and values of an organisation is essential.

For example, there's no point throwing your hat into the ring for a position on the board of a sports club if you aren't particularly interested in that sport! Or perhaps vying for a position on the board of a large commercial board if you struggle with profit-driven business models.

Another consideration when assessing a prospective board role is geographical experience and the contextual understanding of matters. Organisations have varying presence and operate within different realms and jurisdictions. For example, whilst some multinational companies and not-for-profit organisations have significant international operations, other organisations operate within smaller, well-defined local community boundaries.

One's knowledge of the nature and type of operations on a local, regional, national or global scale is very relevant. Whether attained personally or professionally, appreciating the shape, size and reach of organisations is valuable to informing your potential pathways to the boardroom. Hence, what type of board you'll target at any particular point in time.

Given you've learnt about the different types of boards, I'd like to consolidate this thinking around board pathways and careers for you. I'm going to share something new with you which will help you better appreciate the diversity of boards, their roles and responsibilities.

I've developed a tool for you to be able to plot your sector and geographical experience, allowing you to identify possible starting points, make connections and identify pathways for your board journey.

I'd like to introduce you to the 'BoardSpectrum'! A little cheesy in title but informative and well-described.

The BoardSpectrum (Figure 5) is an infographic depiction which I've developed to capture and represent, in a simple format, the size/scale and type/nature of organisations, and their geographical reach. It is a tool to help you classify and categorise entities so you can identify where you best align, given your set of skills, background and experience.

The greatest benefit with this concept is that you can plot your journey to date and extrapolate other suitable pathways for boards and committee roles. The BoardSpectrum also helps to reinforce that it's not always one board model which fits all, given the various factors involved.

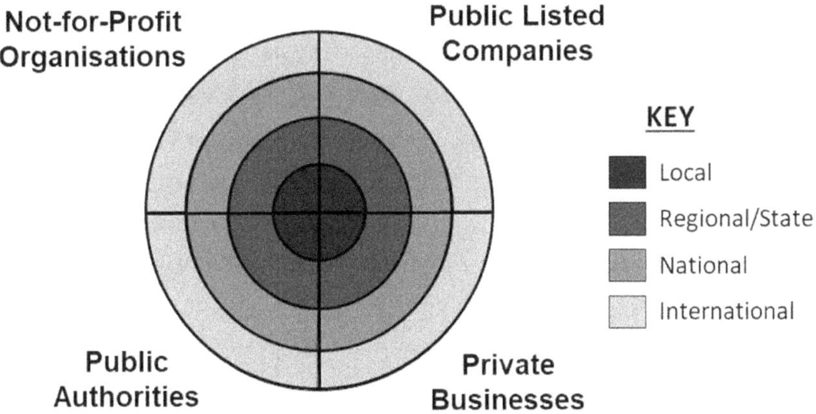

Figure 5: The BoardSpectrum

How to interpret the BoardSpectrum:

1. Quadrants: Each quadrant represents the different types of organisations (not-for-profit, public authorities, private businesses and public listed companies).

2. Rings: The circle and layers of rings represent the nature and scale of geographies e.g. the inner circle represents a local community and the outer ring represents a global scale. See Table 3 for an explanation of each of the layers.

Rings	Geographical Reach of Rings	Description of Rings
Centre/First	Local	The core represents the local level, representative of a small community with clear or unclear boundaries. For example, a school council with a defined site or a local community with undefined boundaries.
Second	Regional/State	Broader geographical area with either unclear regional boundaries or strict state-based boundaries. For example, a state road authority has defined boundaries whereas a tourist area may cover an approximated area.
Third	National	Country-based area with clear boundaries. Outreach extends across an individual country, servicing or distributing within a single nation. For example, a nation-wide retailer.
Fourth/ Outer	International	International presence across multiple countries or continents across the world. For example, a manufacturer with global product distribution hubs.

Table 3: Geographical descriptions

Using the BoardSpectrum to observe the breakdown of organisations helps highlight the various skill sets required for the different contexts in which entities operate. Please note though, this tool is not intended to be rigid, but rather an indicative guide for segmentation, helping you find your best alignments to better focus your energies and efforts.

'How do I use the BoardSpectrum?' Easy. At a glance but without a great deal of analysis, match up your sector experience to the relevant quadrant/s and your geographical reach to the ring/s. You may not fit into just one segment but perhaps span across two or three or more, depending on your background. From those points, your preferred pathways will be those within the relevant quadrant or around the corresponding ring.

Your direction

I hope this has given you some confidence in understanding what types of boards there are on a broad scale and what they are looking for in a non-executive director. I want to make sure you're not only equipped with the essentials, but that you can head in a direction with reasonable expectations.

Maybe you're thinking, 'Oh, this is starting to feel really serious'? Yes, it might seem like that, but have no fear! How often have you become nervous when you've ventured outside your comfort zone and started to really work on an important goal?

Think back to Chapter 1 and what you committed to. Turn that concern into excitement and maintain that positive mindset. Think about how far you've come in this journey already. Previously, you may have had little or no idea about boards but instinctively knew you had to explore it further.

You're embarking on a whole new journey and potentially a long, life-changing one. You won't always know what lies ahead but you can only do your best in preparing. You never know where things will go!

Whilst you'll need to give conscious thought and energy to your preparations, remember not to overthink it. Give due respect to your intuition and instinct. This will be one of your most valuable skills – putting faith in your directions and decisions.

For me, my journey has led down a path of sitting on boards, guiding boards and helping those involved. I provide support to groups and individuals across all aspects of board matters. Helping those in the board space is not where I expected my journey would go, however this is how my path has evolved.

Your board pathway

In learning about the BoardSpectrum, hopefully you're more appreciative of the range in boards and committees out there screaming out for people with core skills, relevant skills and future skills to join them.

To complement this step in appreciating the essentials needed for the various types of boards, let's now take a look at you specifically. The following chapters will enable you to further refine your target destinations and pathways by reaching into, drawing out and understanding your own unique set of qualities.

In Chapter 5, you will step through a process to refine your thinking about yourself, your capabilities and capacities. You'll take a look at your own skills and attributes to better match yourself to the right type of board. You will undertake a personal scan that you can use to cross reference and reconcile with your plotting and thinking on the BoardSpectrum.

The process will help you further build confidence, develop focus, funnel your energies and stay on track without wasting unnecessary time and effort. Are you ready?

Chapter 4 Checklist

- ☐ Board skills
- ☐ Future skills
- ☐ Board pathways
- ☐ On to Chapter 5

5

PASSENGER SCAN

'Wow, can you believe it? I had no idea they could do that!' How many times have you heard someone say this?

I believe everyone has something that they are good at. It may be known or unknown, perhaps not yet developed or maybe not yet unleashed. A natural streak, ability, craft or talent which makes someone unique and helps define them – whether it be art, sport, academia, nurturing, business, science or something else.

Most importantly, none of these capabilities in different areas are any better than others. This is just what makes each of us individual and truly unique, enriching society and giving depth and diversity.

My mother is a great example of having a natural hidden talent, which was unknown for many years. As a young woman, she neglected an artistic urge. She felt it wasn't her place as an artist, as her older sister was renowned as the talented sketcher and painter of the family.

Many years later, in her mid-sixties, my mother intuitively started sketching. She revelled in the joy and after a number of hours, stood back to view what she had created. She had drawn an amazing portrait. She and the family had no idea that her suppressed talent could have produced such amazing results. Lucky she followed her heart and instinct!

I love this story as it highlights how we can have hidden talents that sometimes just need the right opportunity to shine. What about the case where we underestimate ourselves and our own capabilities, where others can see more in us than we give ourselves credit for? Of course, there's also the opposing case, where some people think more of themselves than their capability allows.

This concept is best explained by the Johari Window Model, shown in Figure 6. This was developed in 1955 by two American psychologists, Joseph Luft and Harry Ingham from the University of California.

The model represents what we know and don't know about ourselves, and what others know or don't know about us as individuals. It helps give insight into who we are, how we are perceived by others and therefore how we interact with the world.

The four quadrants on the opposite page highlight the four forms of 'Self' (Life, 2015):

- Open/Public Self: what you and others know about you
- Blind Self: what others know about you but you don't
- Hidden/Private Self: what others don't know about you but you do
- Undiscovered/Unknown Self: what neither you nor others know about you.

Which of these concepts do you think apply to yourself or others you know?

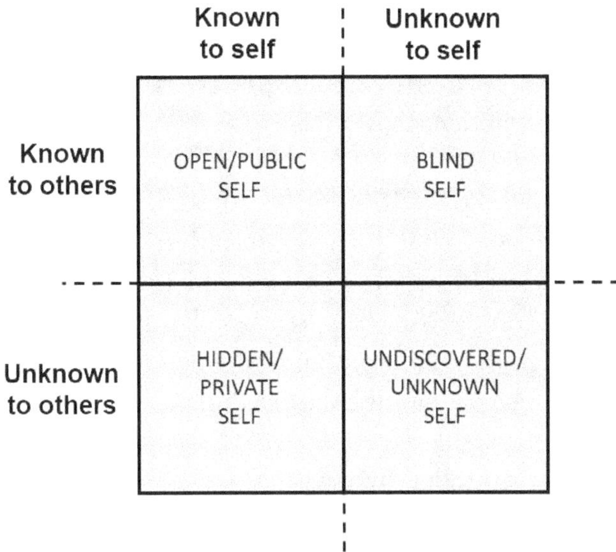

Figure 6: The Johari Window Model

Self-awareness

So, guess what? It's time to refocus on you again. Yes, you wholeheartedly, warts and all! The purpose is for you to better understand who you are, what makes you tick, what's important to you, what you excel at, and what you can truly offer.

In this chapter, you will continue your journey of self-discovery to focus on your talents, the knowledge you've gained, and the skills and capabilities you've developed.

Whether you feel comfortable about it or not, self-awareness is a concept that as a prospective board member, you definitely need to grasp. Being self-aware is about having conscious knowledge of one's own character and feelings, and the capacity to appreciate and apply your whole self. Your personality, characteristics, attitudes, beliefs and emotions are just some of the aspects that make you unique, and influence how you interact with others and relate with the world around you.

Personal characteristics play a big role in our behaviour and practices. As you may know, this is a case of both nature and nurture – those attributes we are born with and those traits which we develop through our life experience.

Given we take our whole self to the boardroom, it is helpful to have this self-knowledge. Having an appreciation of one's attributes provides insight into how you can best add value to a board, and its organisational objectives and outcomes. Qualities brought to the table by each member, underpin and enhance the board with rich discussion, deliberation and decision-making.

Before you can get your boarding pass and take flight, your passenger details have to be known. In Chapter 2, you explored your drivers, desires, passions, objectives and purpose, but this time, your focus is on your capabilities and capacities. I'd like to help you develop your awareness to clearly understand your offering. This will also help you confirm your alignment to various types of boards, organisations, industries and sectors.

This process is intended to be enlightening and empowering rather than a heavy gap analysis. Be prepared: there will be gaps. That's the reality. Remember, no one is an expert on everything! You'll benefit from a clearer set of thoughts, strengths and greater sense of self. You'll refine your offering, become more focused and save time by better understanding yourself and your value proposition.

The process you're about to embark on will be unique to you. You will fully appreciate your own set of qualities, individual strengths, skills, attributes, capabilities and capacities. It may not be the easiest of processes and what you discover might challenge you, but that's a good thing.

The gift is that you will develop greater clarity and ultimately confidence with this enhanced insight. You will be enriched with the understanding of what environments you thrive in.

Self-reflection

Your personal passenger scan and self-awareness journey will begin with self-reflection. Take some action for yourself now! Set a time for a date with yourself. Open your calendar and allocate a couple of hours in a quiet relaxing place. During your session, consider, pose and answer questions about what makes up you and creates your story. Ask, reflect, think, imagine and answer.

Reflect on yourself holistically, paying attention to the skills that you hold naturally and also those which you have attained along on your journey to date. Skills may be personal or professional ones which you have developed. Pay particular attention to what makes you unique.

Think in totality. Consider your dreams, passions, interests, values and beliefs outside of your family and career. Be sure to pay attention to your standout strengths and standout weaknesses.

Remember, it doesn't matter where these skills have derived from, providing they can be competently applied. Whilst qualifications are great, knowledge, understanding, context and application are key aspects which need to be explored.

You may be someone who doesn't necessarily have a qualification, but rather life skills developed and proven by relevant experience. Perhaps you've built a reputation based on or around a unique set of skills or become known for something in particular?

Attributes may be natural or learned and developed with practice. Other qualities or attributes may be unusual or a bit outside the box. They're a set of personalised aspects specifically related to your character, work and life experiences, or derived from once-off or repeated experiences.

Your personal insight may have been either positive or negative, but unexpected, such as personal trauma or sickness. Or on the flipside, maybe you've had an amazing life-changing experience, like inventing a product which suddenly exploded in demand and sales.

What is it that you can offer to a board? What is your unique package of attributes? Is it that you have specialised knowledge? Have you achieved something extraordinary? How did you overcome all odds? What is your particular experience? Really get to know and understand yourself to define your individual value to a board.

Consider your specialist knowledge, and your understanding and application of it. Make sure you reflect across all areas of your life, irrespective of whether your experience was from paid work, volunteer roles or personal activities. That way, you can concisely share this with others of how you can be of greatest benefit to a board and achieve effective outcomes on the behalf of others.

Personal attributes

What are your hard skills? How about your technical skills? Perhaps you've worked as a nurse or carer, social worker, educator, scientist, engineer, farmer, vet, builder or some other area of expertise that requires a specific set of technical skills.

What are your business or administrative skills? For example, do you know how to manage finances, implement governance, develop a strategy, evaluate a policy?

Consider your soft skills. How do you best communicate? Are you attentive? What about your values?

One's morals and ethics are a significant part of personal characteristics which are taken to the boardroom.

As noted earlier in this chapter, the case may also be that others can see more to us than we can ourselves. One of my favourite sayings is 'You can't see the forest for the trees!'

The saying suggests that one can be so distracted by the details surrounding them (i.e. the trees) that the broader context is overlooked.

I'm a firm believer that, no matter how good you are at something, there are times when it can be difficult for you to fully appreciate what's going on around you. Hence, you may be unaware of certain aspects which are otherwise obvious to others.

The Johari Window Model supports this thinking. Bearing this in mind, consider seeking some feedback or input from others who know you personally and/or professionally to gain further insight as a part of this reflective process.

External feedback can shed further light. Sometimes other people's insights can help us better understand ourselves, but make sure you choose the right people to ask for feedback. Be sure they're ok with the idea of having to be critical and honest. This process will help you gain a more diverse perspective.

Be sure to ask some hard questions and be prepared to potentially face some tough feedback. If the comments are completely different to what you think, take the time to understand why.

Through your open-mindedness, be willing to understand and accept the feedback as constructive as it will help you in many ways. In any case, maintain a sense of grounding and level-headedness.

It's important in your self-reflection process to try not give yourself the answers you think you and others want to hear. Be completely upfront, even raw, with yourself. Honesty is not going to hold you back. Equally, don't be too critical!

If you're someone who doesn't like confronting conversations, you'll need to get over that quickly. The achievement of your goal of being at the board table depends on your ability to communicate effectively, and with confidence and maturity.

This is all part of the learning and enlightenment process – it is not to be feared but embraced. Take the opportunity to step up and rise to the occasion with strength. In order to develop yourself, you may need to grow some thick skin, and as a board member, you may need this at times.

Personal clarity

How did you go? Are you finding this task challenging or rewarding? Anything you're surprised about? Feel deficient in? Are your assumptions realistic or in your mind? Are these thoughts holding you back?

Sometimes we can be awfully unfair, placing limitations on ourselves. Seeking external help from a third party can help alleviate some of these inner, unjustified views and concerns. Best to be open-minded, conscious and aware rather than ignorant to self, others and opportunities.

When I sat down and did this process a few years ago, I was pleasantly surprised with the skills and attributes I had acquired (whilst acknowledging there were a few things I also needed to work on). I had previously continued to take a traditional business approach and reflect on myself only in a professional sense. Therefore, I had neglected much of the personal journey I had ventured down and the subsequent development that had taken place in that space.

In doing this reflection, I also realised that my journey had overcome what others may have seen as barriers.

As I mentioned, I was young when I got my first board role. I wasn't tall – under five foot in fact! I had a boss at the time (who rarely stepped out of his comfort zone) who said to me, 'You know you'll never make it … because of your stature.'

This was an interesting moment! In the first instance, I was uncertain about where he thought I was particularly heading to. I was also gobsmacked he'd actually said that and thought that my height was a barrier!

I knew I was little, and was always told I was little but I never really felt little. The only true time I felt small was recently when my first child grew bigger than me and then when I met a man who was seven-foot-tall!

I was no CEO when I landed my first board role. I was pregnant and then a young mother. I was a female engineer and there weren't many of us around nor were there many women on boards at the time.

All of these factors combined (back then) didn't really align with the traditional image of a board member. I could have easily created stories and barriers in my mind from those comments which would have meant that there was no way I would've sought board work. My heart was calling it, and it was the trust in my drive that mattered.

Perceived barriers are there to challenge you and only you can decide if they're going to keep you out. I only just passed English in Year 12, and yet here I am writing a book!

What narrative are you telling yourself? If I told myself stories like, 'I can't be on a board because I'm short' or 'I can't write a book because I've always been bad at English', then you wouldn't be reading this right now. It has been the acknowledgement of being true to myself and listening to the urge to get my message out which has driven me.

Traditional perceptions and expectations have changed and will continue to. Thank you Jacinda Ardern! Elected Prime Minister of New Zealand in 2017 at age 37, Jacinda was unmarried, fell pregnant shortly after being elected to Office and later became engaged to marry her partner.

A leader full of admirable skills and attributes, making her one of the most progressive decision-makers in the world. Someone who is approachable, inclusive, decisive and forward-thinking. Whose actions are busting old moulds. I'm guessing she didn't say to herself, 'I'm too young to be Prime Minister!'

My point for highlighting this is for you to be true to you. Be the authentic you. Place trust in yourself, your instinct and your insights. There is no need to let barriers hold you back from gaining clarity about your story, offering, and value proposition.

Sometimes we don't realise the specialist skills and expertise we've developed over time or that we have something substantial to offer. I came to realise my level of knowledge and understanding of board work from the many questions from others about boards.

Both individuals and boards of varying types have sought my guidance. As a result, I've been involved in all sorts of projects and matters including board performance, organisational set up and structure, strategic planning and priorities, policy development, future directions and sustainability, risk management and mitigation, and governance reviews.

Clients have included established boards, CEOs and senior executives, experienced non-executive directors, new and aspiring directors, business owners, founders and community groups.

What have you come to realise as you go through this self-awareness process? What comes to mind for you? What's unique to you? Like me, you will have developed certain skills, specialist knowledge and understanding. Something you can pull together into a unique package to communicate to others.

New insights

One thing that can happen at the end of this process is that the results can be different to those you expected. Sitting there, you may have just finished your self-reflection and you might feel completely deflated and demoralised. Equally, you may have impressed yourself.

This is the awakening and enlightening process all rolled into one. It is a holistic self-reflection because that is who you take to the boardroom. Whatever you discover, whatever you find, go with it. Allow this new information to guide you.

Be sure to undertake this process again regularly, especially if you've had some pivotal points in your life, either personally or professionally. Remember we constantly grow, and our individual perspectives change with life experiences, so it's good to get the updated snapshot.

At this stage, you need to take a step on the path and allow it to be redirected, just as you would with any journey, be it career or life. As you venture along, you'll set goals which will stretch you, then you'll reassess and reset your direction. This iterative approach will help to take you beyond where you thought you could ever go.

Having completed your personal scan, you should now better appreciate not only your purpose and direction, but what industry and what sector best aligns with you. Hopefully you have also built confidence around your individual offering by gaining a full insight into your range of attributes, e.g. your technical skills, business skills, personal skills and interpersonal skills.

Your personal scan should also provide you with a far greater sense of who you are, what you want to achieve and where you can potentially fly to. Some of your unknowns may even become knowns. You now know more about what makes you unique and where to best funnel your energies.

Importantly, you have identified a unique package. A personal set of skills which can contribute to an overall mix, capability and effectiveness of a board as a collective. Be comforted too that you will further develop well-rounded skills as you grow personally and professionally with roles, experience and lifelong learning.

If a niggling voice is saying something like, 'I don't have all the skills …', remember it's not a matter of being an expert at everything. Equally, you don't have to fit into all the quadrants and rings of the BoardSpectrum.

After watching the documentary, *The Will to Fly* (no pun intended but it does fit well), at a fundraiser evening, I was fortunate to witness the subject of the film, aerial skier and Olympian Lydia Lassila, address a room of people. She shared her hopes and dreams from when she was a child right through to her achievements as an adult, elite athlete, businesswoman, wife and mother.

Lydia's drive and determination to leave a legacy was incredible. Despite having already won an Olympic gold medal in aerial skiing, she wanted to pave the way for other sportswomen to achieve more. She worked hard on her aerial skills, eventually achieving feats which no other woman in the world had done before.

Lydia had a personal vision, an instinct, an urge and a desire, alongside a whole lot of determination, self-belief and pure guts to push boundaries. She led the way, breaking down the perceived limitations of the sport, and inspiring and encouraging other women to aim higher … literally.

Competing and landing a jump only previously achieved by males, Lydia demonstrated what can be done. As a result, the same aerial tricks are now often performed by other female aerialists. She is a true champion!

Lydia's incredible efforts and achievements are the epitome of what can result from pushing with mindsets, commitment, confidence, self-belief and instinct. Whilst Lydia took a flying trip to the Olympics, the rest of her journey took just as much courage.

Following the movie, we purchased a copy of Lydia's book *The Will to Fly*. She signed a personal message and scribed the following words to my children inside the front cover. It was such an inspiring moment for the next generation.

Face your fears and live your dreams!
– Lydia Lassila,
Olympian

New understanding

A key benefit of this self-reflection and assessment is understanding one's attributes and those which will lead you to develop your unique value proposition. We will explore the construction of this in the next chapter.

If joining a board is the destination your heart is choosing, there's no holding back! You know who you are, even though others may not yet. Let's take your insights and build on this to develop a profile so you can let the world get to know you.

You now have the confidence of what you personally have to offer. I hope you realise you have some of the necessary attributes to get a board position, not just at some point in the future, but now!

When is the right time to start? Immediately! Why wait?

Chapter 5 Checklist

- ☐ Technical skills
- ☐ Business skills
- ☐ Personal skills
- ☐ Interpersonal skills
- ☐ On to Chapter 6

6

PASSENGER PROFILE

You may have heard the term 'C-suite'?

What this is referring to is the 'C-level' of organisational positions or senior executive roles known as the 'Chief' positions, for example, the Chief Executive Officer (CEO), Chief Operating Officer (COO) and Chief Financial Officer (CFO). This has often been considered the training ground, door mat and departure lounge for the board! Given this link at the strategic level of the organisation, many perceive boards as exclusive and/or elitist.

Rightly so, there are many boards where it is essential to have a degree of experience. However, as the BoardSpectrum highlights, board positions are about having relevant experience and there are plenty of boards which don't require quite the same level of advanced skills.

Certainly, who would want their banking controlled by a group of directors who didn't know how to manage millions or billions of dollars? The ideal objective for a board and its stakeholders is to attract the right person with the right skills, at right time, for the right reason!

The value I took to the board was a quietly known set of skills. They developed a reputation on their own which translated into more board opportunities and reappointments as a board member. I hadn't been a C-level officer before becoming a non-executive director but after eight different boards and committees, my unique value proposition strengthened and my story had further developed.

Now the emphasis is on you. It's time to create and refine your personal story; your profile.

What's your value? What's your unique proposition to the world? Your story too will continue to evolve and morph into a new narrative after each leg of your journey.

Once you've defined your personal story, you'll walk away with a greater sense of confidence in yourself and be comfortable in projecting your story out into the world in various formats: online, offline and in person. This will become the foundation that you will draw upon, customise and use to inform other documentation when searching for a board position. It may even be useful for other purposes such as job applications, social media or maybe a website.

Your value

You've just put yourself through a gruelling process to learn and appreciate your skills and offerings. You can now use these insights to develop your personal profile that introduces you and leaves others with a glowing impression of you.

Imagine being number one in the eyes of any board looking for a new member. Not only that, imagine that your profile and pitch out in the public domain showcases who you really are, shares your authenticity and highlights the value you bring.

By the end of this chapter, you'll gain an appreciation for your own unique story. The purpose is to build your narrative, make it relevant and align yourself and your efforts with what makes you tick. Your personal story will be articulated in a way that reflects you, your journey to date and where you're heading. Your story will be a reflection of all that you are, who you are, what you stand for and what you can offer.

The benefit is that both you and others will better understand and appreciate you in your entirety. This will be something which presents you and provides a convincing pitch for maximum impact. Most importantly, you will be able to make sure that all your forms of communication (online, offline and face-to-face), are consistent and aligned.

Projecting your personal narrative is the process of sharing your background, achievements, values and directions with others. Similar to an organisation, call it your 'brand' or 'image'. How you look, how you sound, your body language, what you write and your vibe – it all creates that overall sense that people get from you and contributes to the package of information making up your brand.

Over time and with an increase in digital communication, there has been a shift to sharing the reality of our daily lives. This social movement seems to be helping with the acceptance of individuality.

I'd like to think this trend of acceptance will continue into the future. I relish the idea that there is growing appreciation and trust for those representing their whole selves rather than just one side of their character. At the end of the day, this is what walks into the boardroom.

Over time, we develop, grow and change. We take on new personal and/or professional adventures for different reasons, leading us down different roads. At various points along the way, we transcend in our thinking.

We change in how we look and how we project outwards and become an updated version of ourselves.

I expect you've noticed this in yourself or those around you? Adjustments in perceptions, outlook, opinions, clothing and hair for example, reflecting an evolving individual you and your true style with authenticity and transparency.

People have come to know me for my curly hair. As a child I was teased a lot about it. I would tie my hair back, straighten it – anything to reduce the volume of curls protruding from my head. I even did it in the 80s when perms were the trend! But I constantly heard, 'People pay good money to get their hair looking like yours!' I'd be well off if I had a dollar for every time I heard that. Or for every time I was called Shirley Temple or Nicole Kidman!

Funnily enough though, those curls were a signature characteristic which somewhat defined my individuality. 'Do you know Stacey?' 'She's the short one with the curly hair, right?' Sadly, it took too long to fully appreciate what I had!

What is your persona and individual style? What are you known for? Maybe it's not what you look like but other factors that you are known for? Some personal capability? What contributes to your authenticity? These questions will help you form the basis of your unique story and define your image and your brand.

Think about some people you know. What are they known for? Why do people go to them for help? What about some high-profile individuals – what are they known for? Is it for good or bad reasons? I'm sure you can think of some examples.

Your impact

An important aspect of sharing your story is the initial impression you give people. That initial contact can play a big part in how you're perceived, and you want to get this right from the outset. Ideally you want a first impression to reflect the real and genuine you so others gain a good sense of authenticity in which they can relate and connect.

What first impression do you give? What impact do you have? How about when someone doesn't know of you or your story – how do you get others to understand you and what you have to offer? How do you overcome any bias they might have?

While a book should not be judged by its cover, many people are unlikely to read it if the cover is not inviting.

– Anonymous

I love this quote. I can so appreciate it. As someone who has often been underestimated at first glance, this quote highlights what I'm trying to share with you. Sometimes you can't guess what's on the inside as opposed to what you see on the outside.

We all display a front cover. However, these days, it may not be limited to just the three-dimensional one that forms our real life, but potentially the two-dimensional virtual one shared online. The web, online platforms, social media and other forms of digital exposure lead to the development of quasi-public 'book covers'.

Anyone can find out information about you. The reality is that those who view your profile and other details about you will develop certain impressions and perceptions of you. Judgements and opinions about you and your persona are made within seven seconds or even faster (Gibbons, 2018).

Getting past those initial impressions to make an impact is also the role of your story. Boardrooms were once mostly filled with business suits, but you may find boardroom attire quite different these days, as acceptance for individuality increases.

Boards are a combination of personal styles coming together to enhance discussion, deliberations and decisions. Until others know your capabilities, expertise and value, first impressions can play a large part in getting you there in the early stages.

Making an initial impact is a balancing act of these first impressions and telling your story. Making a long-term impact is about you, your value, your contribution and making a difference.

Your story

What's your story to tell? One which reflects you, your characteristics, your qualities and attributes. The benefit of defining this is that you will continue to build on fresh thinking from the last chapter to generate your narrative. Let's get you fully equipped to share who you are and what you can offer so you can put your best foot forward.

To assist with developing the context and framing of your narrative, go back and remind yourself of your reasons for joining a board. See where you're best aligned and which boards you are most suited to according to your experience, skills and knowledge. This will help refine your story, language, destination and pathway.

Consider the outcomes and findings from the last chapter. Those from your reflections and feedback from others. Of what does your overall package comprise? What are your capabilities and attributes, in both your professional capacity as well as your personal capacity? What's your character and individual style? Where you can really add value?

There's no need to hide from your achievements. Be realistic, but equally don't overexaggerate. We can often underestimate ourselves, so it's important to be level minded and call it for what it is.

Some people aren't comfortable sharing their capabilities and accomplishments, which means that their story doesn't reflect their true character and journey. Equally, some embellish their story only to get caught out later. Those who overestimate their capabilities will soon be found out if there's not a match.

Be honest and transparent as people aren't stupid. Whilst there is wriggle room and acceptance for some inexperience, learning and development, there's no room to be misleading.

You are building a platform of credibility and reliability around the present and authentic you. For some, this can take some practise and if you need to improve on this, now is a good time to start!

In putting your story together, what ideas are taking shape? What are the themes? Does it genuinely reflect the true you? Consider how it compares to the story you've been telling yourself.

What an exciting time! A pivotal point which frames your strengths, passions and values in a format you can share. Your personal story and profile are a summary of you at this point in time.

Your narrative reflects your personal journey to date and needs to talk about you holistically. For board applications, your story needs to be framed in the context of boards. It needs to highlight and reflect the value you can bring to decision-making, to that particular organisation and to the beneficiaries of its outcomes.

For some, this self-focused process can be both daunting and exhilarating. This is self-appreciation at its best. Be comfortable with your story. Be happy with your story. This is not a complete autobiography, but rather a snapshot of what has shaped you into who you are today. Own it!

Think about the many autobiographies out there. Which ones have you read? My favourite is Richard Branson's *Losing My Virginity*. Despite the risqué title, it was a great read! Mr Branson is someone who has carved out his own story by remaining genuine, stepping beyond his comfort zone and taking risks – an approach we can all learn from.

If you're struggling with putting everything together, ask for help from someone you can trust. A third party can help shed light and guide you to make progress. An independent person may also help tell your story objectively without the emotional attachment. They can ask the hard questions, find the pieces and fit them together.

Imagine the sense of relief when your story comes together – potentially mind blowing and empowering. I'd like you to get to the point where you confidently say, believe and accept 'Wow, that really is who I am and what I stand for'. Some true words of self-realisation.

Your passenger profile is a concise and succinct statement about who you are and what you offer. Once you've completed your profile description and you're happy with it, you can use some or all of the content to update any public profile summaries or introductions.

You may have found the process outlined in this chapter challenging or confronting. Being able to compile the various elements together in a comprehensive narrative can be difficult, especially when we're talking about ourselves. You wouldn't be the first to feel uncomfortable with trying to both consolidate and portray your own story.

Think of me writing this book and telling my story. I've had to overcome many mindset limitations to share all of this with you! This has been a huge step out for me, and it is nerve wracking to think this will be out for the world to see, warts and all. I wouldn't say I'm the world's greatest writer, but I've given it a go! I've learnt plenty from this first-time experience and if I chose to do it again, I expect it would be a lot different.

As I've already shared, writing a book was something I really wanted to do 'one day'. That day eventually arrived when I decided to go with my heart and just start framing up what was sitting in my mind. I had no idea how to execute such a task, yet it has been a process I've slowly and steadily navigated in the spirit of continuous learning and improvement.

Your offer

My hope for you is that this chapter has given you the benefit of understanding yourself, realising your value, recognising your capabilities and learning how to form your own personal story. You may have even learnt more about yourself. My hope is that you have also come to feel comfortable and confident enough to pitch yourself, not just as an aspiring director, but as a prospective director.

As you journey along your path, be sure to regularly go back and update your profile. Make sure your narrative reflects the shiny, new updated version of you. Keep it current and keep it fresh.

With your profile complete and a good sense of direction, you're nearly ready to prepare for launch. The time has come come to be bold! It's time to get out there so that other people start to learn who you really are and what you can bring to the boardroom.

With your combined personal and professional statement of experience, you can take this description in hand for your next step in Chapter 7. Armed with a clear mind, you can step up into the world of boards.

Chapter 6 Checklist

- ☐ Personal value
- ☐ Personal story
- ☐ Personal profile
- ☐ On to Chapter 7

7

NAVIGATION

'Errr … Umm … Hmmm …'

Why the hesitation? Not sure what to expect? Not sure where to head for further information? Unsure how to take that first step? Not sure if you fit? Perhaps still uncertain if you are good enough to play in this space?

Have you heard the saying, 'A confused mind will always say no'? I've seen many people not progress or give up because they're not sure which way to go or what to do. Sometimes things can appear all too hard when it comes to making a decision, that it can appear easier not to make one or leave it for another day. Can you relate?

In this chapter, I'd like to help you read the compass, take a step forward and navigate the world of boards. You may feel outside of your comfort zone and think you're not ready for it but when it comes to tomorrow, you'll wish you started today. I can encourage you but ultimately you have to be the one to push yourself into the unknown!

Until you try, you don't know what you can't do.
- Henry James,
author

Every great outcome starts with an idea and every great journey starts with a step. You want to funnel your precious energies into action. You've learnt about yourself so far and now you can learn more about boards and committees. The focus in this chapter is on how and where to gain general information to build a bigger base of board knowledge.

This chapter is aimed at directing you to finding the answers to the many other questions you have about boards, positions and their business. This will help you take a deeper look into learning more about the activities, lingo and the context of board work, board talk and boardroom matters. You'll understand where to go to gain greater insight and clarity so that you can make more educated decisions.

This process will help you to identify what else you want to learn, what other learning tools you may wish to acquire and where to find it. The benefit is that your thoughts will be more refined, you'll be more knowledgeable and more confident to navigate your new journey. Hopefully, you will have an overwhelming sense of, 'Now I get it!'

So let's go exploring. Let's begin weaving through the world of boards and committees so you can really understand what's involved.

Research

One of the most important attributes of a non-executive director is the ability to independently undertake research. Knowing where to go hunting for information, and knowing what to do with it once you've got it. This is to help you to make independent decisions – the key responsibility of a board member.

Whilst it's important to listen and appreciate other's viewpoints, it is imperative that you do your own research to help you form your own views. This begins early even when you're not on a board, as you grow your general knowledge about the inner workings of boards and their business.

This phase becomes iterative; following your own compass. First you start with an idea, then questions, then answers, then more ideas, more questions and then more answers. Navigating this new pathway is not dissimilar to looking for a job or developing new innovations, involving a constant journey of exploration, understanding and refinement.

There are many methods to building and developing your own database. Your personal research and development is not limited to any one source. It now encompasses a wide range of information formats and avenues for investigation which are now instantly available and readily accessible.

Whilst online research is probably the easiest, there are many other formats and places to obtain information. I'd like to encourage you to explore more broadly. Find opportunities to read hardcopy books and journals in the local library or university, or perhaps attend different events. To be a well-rounded board-being, it is important to have an appreciation of the diverse means of hunting and gathering information.

Start with the basics and keep it simple. Initially familiarise yourself and observe; perhaps make a list of questions about things you want to know more about. What is vital is that you don't create a situation of paralysis by analysis. Too much exploration and data collection can become overwhelming and lead you to inaction. Keep it simple and build on what you've learnt so far and know that there is plenty of time ahead to continue your research.

To begin, you may find value in some general reading, exposing yourself to all types of boards and committees. Understand some of the variations in structure and requirements, as highlighted on the BoardSpectrum. You may find yourself narrowing your search depending on your experience, interest and curiosity.

Again, ensure this research has purpose and is building knowledge for momentum, not stagnation. Explore relevant online communications including websites and social media. What you want to look at is a good cross section of information relating to boards e.g. articles, announcements, market updates and business newsletters. See what general materials you can find.

Navigating this new world may be a challenge and lead to information overload. A tip: if you're starting to feel overwhelmed, avoid memorising the details of everything you consume and just pick up on key points. You don't want to be in a state of flux while you're building your confidence in this introductory phase. Be persistent without setting unreasonable timeframes for this step. Allow yourself the time you need to reflect and enjoy this new knowledge and space.

Once you are feeling like you're grasping the concepts, focus on the types of boards and committees which showed up in your BoardSpectrum plot. This will help keep your research streamlined and digestible so that it is not too overwhelming. This phase and process aims to build your confidence step-by-step, rather than feeding you so much that you can't manage the meal!

Connections

Building an information bank isn't just a reading exercise. Going to events and meeting people can also be a good means of learning, and for others to learn about you. There are plenty of opportunities you can get engaged in to help you.

You may decide you'd like to attend information sessions, networking events, and workshops targeted at non-executive directors and/or boards. These offer you the chance to meet people and learn all sorts of aspects about board matters. You may even consider attending local council meetings or an Annual General Meeting (AGM) in which you're a shareholder. You don't have to participate, just observe if you wish.

Each year there is a key learning and networking event I go to. I extend my knowledge from the information presented, by the questions asked, and the responses received to those questions. The added bonus of this event is that it allows me to meet up with former colleagues and others I know, as well as meeting new people.

I've found some opportunities invaluable. When engaging in face-to-face conversations, I've gained greater insight, often learnt something new and met some of the most amazing people. You never know what you'll come away with or who you'll come across, but sometimes you just need to get out of your comfort zone to allow for new experiences to occur.

I recall an event I went to, held at Government House in Melbourne. The seating was unallocated and I found myself sitting in the centre of a few hundred attendees.

During a break in proceedings, the lady beside me struck up a conversation. Our initial interaction was cut short when the formalities recommenced. When the event finished, we resumed our conversation and became so engrossed in our discussion that we ended up being amongst the last to leave. A coincidental meeting I wouldn't have expected.

This lady was inspirational. I was wowed by her experience and resilience, and she was equally fascinated by my achievements as a young non-executive director, and my work with boards. This was our common ground, as my new acquaintance had also served numerous terms on various boards and committees. We shared stories and exchanged details.

There was something I learnt during our time together that day that blew me away.

My new acquaintance was older than me by a number of years and, from what I could ascertain, she was strong, renowned and respected. She had achieved a significant award honouring her efforts and contributions to society. However, our conversation made me realise that no matter your achievements in career or life, you're not precluded from life's adversities.

It's a sad reality that tragedy can strike anyone. I learnt that this lady, who had given so much, had as a mother endured losing one of her children in the most unexpected way (in an overseas terrorist attack). As she told me her story, my heart sank and I choked up as I learnt the family's circumstances and ongoing aftermath that followed this event.

Her story exemplifies that you never really know what's around the corner in life. What I learnt from this truly inspirational woman's insight and life experience is that you've got to be ready to give everything your most, all of the time. There will be good days and there will be bad days, but it's how you pick yourself up that will define you and your end point.

Step out, move down the path and refine your direction as you go. This lady's ability to do exactly this was incredibly moving.

Your compass might spin around and out of control from time to time, but you can always push the reset button to get back on track. Resetting plays an incredible part in rethinking and repositioning your journey to your preferred destination.

Whilst some meetings like this can be unexpected, of course others will be intentional. This will be part of the conscious navigation of your board journey. There may be certain people that you would like to be introduced to or meet as you may have some burning questions for them. Most people are happy to help, so reach out to those people in your network to help point you in the right direction.

Meeting others will occur formally and informally, professionally and personally. Whether through direct conversation or online, connecting with others also helps build your profile and shares what you have to offer. It provides the opportunity to let the world know who you are, what you stand for, and what you're seeking, and lets others know you're in the market for a position on a board.

When meeting with others, be sure to focus on them. Ask questions and get to know them. Actively listen and be present. As leadership expert Ty Bennett advocates, 'Be interested not interesting!' (Bennett, 2013).

If you're not sure who you should be approaching or talking to, refer back to your notes and questions as well as checking back in with your goals. Remember to listen to your gut feeling and intuition and ask your mentor or guide for help.

It's like looking for love! It won't happen unless you develop a sense of what you're after and put yourself out there. Researching, browsing, and talking doesn't mean commitment or marriage at this early stage. You're purely exploring to help you on your way.

Reflections

Am I hearing, 'I'm not really a networking person …' and, 'It's really daunting thinking about going to networking events'? I've heard this before and even experienced it myself.

Remember what networking events are. They are there for you to become more informed and meet other people. Everyone else is there for the same reason as you. You belong there as much as anyone else. You wouldn't be the first, nor the last, person who has sought refuge in the toilets, lobby or fiddled with their phone to avoid conversation. True?

Nothing will come of nothing.
- William Shakespeare,
writer, poet and actor

If fear, time, or distance are barriers to making it to face-to-face events, there are options for online networking. Getting involved and connecting with others via virtual forums or groups is now a standard means of learning and sharing information. You can also seek out certain topics and engage with industry conversations via forums and other means online.

Remember, you never know who you could meet, whether it be virtually or personally. How often do you find yourself having unexpected encounters with amazing people? I'm sure you have your own story just like mine. The benefit of meeting the right people is that you could end up in the forefront of their minds for a board position if they're seeking your set of skills and attributes.

Of course, if people haven't heard of you or your unique offering, how can you expect to be contacted? Depending on the appointment process, you could be approached rather than having to compete with others for a seat at the board table. In many cases, boards will seek out the skills needed to fill certain gaps and sometimes tap people on the shoulder to consider joining a board.

'What if I meet someone and leave a bad impression?'. Or perhaps you just have a sense of, 'I really failed to impress'? Many of us are guilty of not putting on our best conversational performance when we really wanted it to matter. Equally, sometimes these bad experiences happen when our gut instinct senses misalignment with the person we are speaking to.

There's no need to beat yourself up. Like many other things in life, reflect on why it didn't go so well and learn from the experience. It's ok to move on after a chance meeting that didn't seem right. You might want to recognise it as something you need to work on and use it as a learning experience.

Sidesteps and setbacks will all be part of your journey, and navigating these along your pathway will make you stronger and more resilient. Chances are it won't be the last time you're not happy with how a conversation or moment in time went but you'll be better positioned to deal with it. You'll equally be better equipped to deliver an improved performance or recognise a poor fit the next time around. A good character will tackle these hiccups and continue on their journey.

I acknowledge that getting out there, outside of your comfort zone, meeting people, joining forums and asking questions can be a real barrier for some. Yet this can be pivotal and transformational in your growth.

When I reflect on my story, I perceived few barriers. I saw potential, and this was my focus. My leap of adventure into the board space (before mandates for females on boards) arose from a belief of where I wanted to funnel my energies to make a difference.

A family member in recent times asked me, 'Stacey, where did your confidence come from, to work in the mines and be on boards?' I had to think about it but I said, 'I focused on where I was heading, and no one ever told me I couldn't!'

I reflected and realised that I:

- Followed my heart
- Believed in my direction
- Knew my capabilities
- Sought and seized opportunities
- Informed myself
- Took a diligence approach

- Committed without financial reward
- Contributed and value-added
- Exercised my independent judgement
- Drew on all I had to offer, personally and professionally.

Given I wanted to be on a board one day, this goal became a subconscious focus. It helped me overcome whatever actual or perceived barriers myself or others may have put in front of me, and thus I was able to stay on track.

My focus on the final destination was key to my confidence and effective navigation. I could easily have said to myself, 'I'm only in my early thirties. I'm female. I'm not an executive. I haven't sat on a board before. I'm not even five foot for goodness sake and my feet don't even touch the floor when I sit at a table, let alone a board table!' But I didn't!

New learnings

No matter your fears, barriers or hiccups in navigating your journey, get ready to ramp it up. Investing time, energy, and efforts into refining your direction and destination will make the path to boarding clearer and easier. Not just for any flight, but for the right flight to the right destination.

Perhaps it's been days, weeks or even months since you started your research. Maybe you've been reading, observing, networking, and discussing all sorts of board matters, and surrounding and submerging yourself in a whole new world?

What I hope is that with all this new insight, you feel confident about your journey ahead and positive about your knowledge and understanding of boards, and where your flight path might lead. I hope that you feel comforted by the fact that pivotal points are a part of the refinement and navigation of your personal journey.

Be aware that some doors open when you knock, yet others will remain closed. Sometimes for good reason, other doors remain shut because it's not the right timing or best fit. Knowing and accepting this approach will help ensure you aren't disappointed.

The next step in your flying blueprint to the boardroom is matching you to the right boards and finding suitable positions for you. In Chapter 8, we explore where you can seek, find and assess suitable board roles so that you can best funnel your energies.

Chapter 7 Checklist

- ☐ Knowledge
- ☐ Understanding
- ☐ Confidence
- ☐ On to Chapter 8

8

PRE-FLIGHT CHECKS

It's likely you have heard the saying, 'It's the journey that matters, not the arrival'. Yet in the case of boards, the arrival point is actually very important – you don't want to end up on just any board or committee.

Both yourself and the board want membership to be a good match. As a tradie would say, 'You need the right tool for the right job!' Sitting on a board making decisions is a privilege, and there's no point wasting your time, effort and resources, and that of anyone else's, if you are not the right fit.

Like planning a holiday, it's best to determine which destination you want to travel to first before you can effectively assess how you're going to get there. Perhaps a pre-flight check will help you make a decision?

In this chapter, you'll learn about what is involved with pre-flight checks, or 'due diligence checks' as they're often referred to. This is to determine if a specific board position is suitable for you and you for it. The benefit is that after gaining greater certainty and clarity around an opportunity, you'll be far more empowered to make an informed judgement.

By the end of the chapter, you will know how to find opportunities, what to be aware of, what specific background research you need to do and how to determine its suitability.

Board positions

How do you go about finding board roles – most importantly, suitable ones? There are many different board appointment processes conducted out there and they vary across industries, sectors, organisations and groups. As a prospective director seeking a role, there are generally two ways you'll find a board role, either via an advertisement or someone contacting you about the role.

The method you'd be most familiar with and what many people undertake, is similar to looking for employment. That task of looking at postings via online noticeboards, advertisements and even notices in newspapers. The headline may read, 'Expressions of Interest', 'Applications' or 'Nominations'. No need to be confused over these terms as they're often used interchangeably yet reflect a similar type of process. Essentially boards are seeking suitable applicants in the marketplace.

Another means of finding out about board positions is through your own network and word-of-mouth. Alternatively, you may be headhunted or tapped on the shoulder and asked to consider a position. You may be approached directly by someone who knows of you, your qualities and your attributes, and believes you may complement an existing skills mix and add value to a certain board.

You may also find board roles when they are promoted for upcoming elections. These are often advertised within membership entities or public offices where there is a regular cycle and standard process associated with the voting in of directors or committee members. The organisation's rules will determine how far and wide the promotion extends.

How new members are appointed centres around these rules or the constitution of the organisation. This key documentation is the overarching governance document outlining instructions for that board and entity. Particular instructions relating to board composition, processes and appointments, are often outlined here and may detail certain formalities or conditions. This may dictate how and where board vacancies are promoted and the subsequent steps in the appointment process.

Irrespective of how you find out about a role, it's important that you ask lots of questions to make an educated decision. Many opportunities have become known to me through various avenues including formal advertisements, email notifications, personal referrals and direct approaches. Each time I posed a range of specific questions to assess the opportunity and determine whether or not to throw my hat in the ring to be considered.

Having been a non-executive director in different sectors and different organisations, I've experienced and observed a range of appointment processes. Once again, there's no 'one-size-fits-all'. You will find significant variations in how such processes are conducted. This may seem confusing, so always seek help and ask for direction from a mentor, or somebody you trust, who is experienced with boards. Receiving guidance at each stage of your journey can be invaluable and will help you arrive at your destination.

Board checks

When you've found a position of interest, whether advertised or through a direct approach, be sure to do your homework. Some background research into the organisation and board is called doing your 'diligence'.

Undertaking a due diligence check is something which allows you to gather specific information to make an educated judgment (much like the task of being a director when you're on the board). As a prospective director, it's necessary to have a good understanding of the organisation, its industrial context, and sectorial relevance.

To confirm expectations about the role, ideally you've been able to get your hands on a position description. This provides details about, and associated with, the position, including conditions and expectations. Before you get too carried away, it's best to firstly confirm that you're actually eligible to be appointed to the board!

Depending on the constitution or governing legislation, you may be void of being able to apply. Any previous imprisonment or criminal charges can obviously impact your chances and opportunities. Eligibility criteria may impose certain conditions such as membership status, geographical location, or even citizenship for example. No board wants a repeat of what might reflect the 2016 – 2017 Australian parliamentary dual citizenship crisis!

In doing your research and becoming more familiar with an organisation, keep in mind another key question: 'Do I have a conflict of interest?' This may also impact your eligibility.

What happens when you're keen on an opportunity and have the right skills as a potential board member, but personal connections and influences cast doubt over your ability to make independent judgements? Perhaps creating a situation where you or others close to you may directly or indirectly benefit from decisions made by the board. Your conflict may not appear significant to some, however your involvement may compromise effective decision-making and outcomes.

What exactly is a conflict of interest, you ask? A conflict of interest (COI) is something which reduces your ability to be independent and exercise your fiduciary duty. You may be considered unsuitable to make decisions on behalf of and for the benefit of others.

There are three types of conflicts of interest. They are:

- Actual: Where there is a real and direct conflict. Where a board member, or their connections, may be advantaged as a result of the board member holding a position on the board.
- Potential: Where there is a risk of conflict occurring in the future that may present a conflict for a board member.
- Perceived: Where conflict by a board member is believed to exist and may cause risk to the organisation.

Conflicts of interest arise through relationships, business interests, property ownership, trust ownership, or company shareholdings for example. They can be presented by circumstances where profits are distributed, or where yourself, your family or friends, may receive a benefit related to the board you're sitting on. The benefits may not necessarily be monetary and may consist of other rewards such as the receipt of products or services. This can cloud your judgement and reduce your independence in making the right decisions on behalf of others.

A conflict of interest doesn't always preclude you from being a part of a board. You may have highly relevant knowledge, insight, and experience, which is valuable to the organisation and can actually lead to more informed decision-making.

Where a conflict is deemed clear and manageable, you may present your information and perspective, and then be excluded from final discussions, decisions, and/or voting. Some boards may request that you leave the room and take no part in any of the discussions nor in the final decision.

Every board deals with conflicts of interest differently within their own set of rules. However, good governance ensures there is total and upfront disclosure. Good practice suggests that conflicts are declared upfront at the point of nomination or application to ensure the circumstances are clearly understood and taken into consideration. This ensures that transparency, honesty, and integrity is upheld throughout the appointment process, subsequent meetings and decision-making.

This disclosure helps to further discover if the opportunity is right for you and if you are right for that board. If the situation cannot be effectively managed, or is controversial or unethical, perhaps consider another opportunity. You want to make sure your first directorship (and subsequent ones, of course) are good experiences.

Board alignment

So how do you know if what you've found is the right opportunity? The right flight? What do you need to consider to further appreciate a potential board opportunity? A good approach is to read key information about the organisation.

This will provide you with insight and an appreciation of the entity, its leadership, direction, culture, and other key aspects. One of the most important considerations to get a handle on is the finances. You want to be comfortable that the organisation is sitting in an acceptable position.

To find further information, look beyond social media and public communications available to appreciate the nuts and bolts. In particular, look at specific business details contained in documents such as business plans, strategic plans, annual reports, financial reports, minutes from meetings, media releases, and announcements. Some of these will be available on the organisation's website.

My tip is to ask purposeful questions, particularly given it is an essential part of a non-executive director's job. This process is giving you practise in asking explicit questions to build on your knowledge and comprehension around a particular matter. If you're unsure, ask more questions. Also query people from the relevant organisation, industry or sector for more insight.

My next tip is to make sure you gather information at a pace which you can digest. Avoid taking on so much that you feel overloaded and overwhelmed. At this stage, you really want to gain an appreciation and snapshot of the health of the organisation, its direction and strategy, culture, sustainability and financial status, to determine if this is the right direction for you.

Remember, the more questions you ask, the more informed you become and the more educated you are. You are then better positioned to form an opinion and contribute to making an educated judgement and decision. There's no need to be concerned if your research results in unexpected outcomes – good, bad or otherwise.

There have been a couple of board roles I've seen advertised over the years, which on the face of them seemed interesting and a good fit. I can recall a time when I was browsing online for a board role when a position popped up on the screen.

I didn't know much about this organisation and wasn't overly familiar with their specific purpose, direction, strategy or operations. I did my due diligence in reading further to understand the business, and in doing so, realised my skills were applicable and relevant. What I didn't anticipate was the limited alignment of this organisation with my personal values, and as a result, I instantly dismissed the opportunity and didn't consider it any further.

Equally, the research I conducted for a board role on another organisation presented a different scenario. This time, the opportunity presented a potential conflict of interest for me. There would not have been sufficient independence from a role on a board I was already fulfilling, so applying wasn't appropriate and pointless.

Sometimes timing can also determine whether you consider the opportunity further. If there's too much going on in your life and you really can't commit, it's okay. Look to get a ticket on the next flight.

At one point, I was really keen to consider another board similar to one I'd previously sat on. In this case though, the level of contribution required was significantly beyond what I was able to reasonably deliver at that time given other commitments.

Another scenario involved me being approached to consider a chair role for a new school in the process of being established. It was at a relatively new organisation with a great vision and great energy. It seemed like a fabulous opportunity. However, my excitement was met with unease. My assessment of the organisation was challenged by not being able to satisfy my first criteria.

This organisation had been operating for a few years and was somewhat still in start-up mode. Despite multiple requests for details, I was unable to satisfactorily ascertain statements regarding the financial performance and position.

I wasn't feeling comfortable about this and my discomfort grew. As a result, despite being interested in helping deliver the amazing vision of this organisation, I had to decline the offer based on the lack of information and growing lack of trust.

The key to having a good board experience is to also make sure you've got some strong and consistent leadership, and a good culture around you. Not long out of university, I worked on a mine site in Western Australia, north of Kalgoorlie. The site was overseen by a South African General Manager (GM). Whilst this gentleman was getting on in life, he held high standards, expected quality and had zero-tolerance for poor work practices.

Despite this GM's daily ritual of a lemon and ginger infusion for the morning meetings, he was a very tough and strict man. There was no such thing as three warnings; it was a case of instant dismissal! The end of morning meetings were always met with his departing words (with a South African accent), 'The fish rots from the head', derived from the quote by British diplomat Sir James Porter.

I still clearly recall his words in my mind. Given it's actually over twenty years on, it's pretty funny to think of his impact! This was our GM's reminder to us about the importance of good leadership, that we as individuals have personal leadership and responsibilities to exercise and uphold within our own roles, in addition to those at the top of the organisation.

The right fit

After reviewing the information you've collected about the organisation of interest, you can ascertain if the opportunity is worth pursuing further. If your gut feeling is positive and your urge is to go for it, then give it the attention it is demanding.

If your gut response isn't favourable, you have no obligation to pursue it any further. Be careful not to get caught up in FOMO (yes, fear of missing out!) moments for all the wrong reasons.

At times, your greatest challenge is likely to involve trying to make sense of head versus heart decisions or vice versa. This is a skill you will master through practice. My biggest tip is not to overanalyse but to make sure the opportunity logically stacks up.

Remember: avoid paralysis by analysis! This can lead to a state of fear, irrational views and inaction. Be sure to maintain the balance. It will be good practise for your decision-making around the board table.

There will be times when, for whatever reason, a board vacancy doesn't suit. Just because a board vacancy is interesting and appeals to you initially, it doesn't mean it's the best fit. Be critical in its suitability. Even if you've over researched a vacancy or commenced an application, it doesn't mean you're obliged to continue to the point of submission, so don't expect yourself to.

Determining early if an opportunity is not the right fit will save you lots of time, effort, and potential heartache. You will also be saving other people's time and energy. You want to apply for roles which suit you and your skill set.

This will give you a greater chance of appointment as well as keeping up your spirits if you haven't yet been successful.

You also want to gain a great sense of fulfilment out of your new role. Any setbacks are a part of the learning process (as with anything in life) and are something worth expecting as a part of this journey. Analogous to a flight, there will be ups and downs.

The right board

To get an indication and sense of suitability for your flight and pre-flight check, you will want to understand your:

- Eligibility and conflicts of interest
- Geographical location and/or experience
- Industry and sector experience
- Organisational experience
- Alignment with values.

You may also want to confirm that the board and organisation satisfies your expectations of:

- Leadership
- Culture and values
- Strategic direction
- Sustainability
- Financial health.

Once you're satisfied with the criteria in your pre-flight checklist, you now need to compile some flight documents. You need some basic documents to confirm your identity, provide some additional details, and highlight your offerings.

In Chapter 9, we'll explore what documentation and information you need to pull together to put your best foot forward! Are you ready?

Chapter 8 Checklist

- ☐ Vacancies
- ☐ Information
- ☐ Suitability
- ☐ On to Chapter 9

9

FLIGHT DOCUMENTS

'Eureka! You've found gold!'

Browsing a vacancy advert, you find a board opportunity which looks promising. At a glance, you look well suited, you're eligible, and have no conflicts of interest. The adrenaline has kicked in!

You click onto their website to immediately start researching the background details. The more you read, the more this organisation and board position really aligns with your values, your purpose, and your skills. Your research shows the organisation has a good track history and a good future vision.

'This is stacking up!' you're thinking. You really want to get involved and contribute to the direction of this organisation and help deliver results. You've found your flight!

If that's the case, it's time to focus on putting together a convincing application.

Be fearless in the pursuit of what sets your soul on fire!
- Jennifer Lee,
screenwriter and film director

In this chapter, I'd like to equip you with the knowledge and understanding of the suite of information you need to package up your documentation.

You'll be able to put your best foot forward with a pointed, customised, and relevant application. That way, you can present all the necessary details to optimise your chances of advancing to the next stage of the appointment process.

Once again, every board member application process is different and can vary from sector to sector and organisation to organisation. Like many things in life, as you go through the entire process, this is when you learn the most. That practical application and open-mindedness to lifelong learning will prove to be invaluable in many ways.

Applying for a board role is not dissimilar to applying for a position or a job of any other type. It's just of a different nature.

You're probably most familiar with the traditional means of nomination involving a letter or summary, a form, a curriculum vitae (CV) or resume, and often a series of criteria to be answered.

With digital disruption and contemporary communications, you may now be asked to provide your details via an online platform, or to present yourself through a video message. But for now, we'll focus on some of the standard expectations and the documentation most often requested.

Board letter

Your value proposition will likely to be in the form of a letter, commonly known as the 'cover letter'. This is your key pitching document and should be tailored to the particular opportunity you're applying for. This formally expresses your interest in the role, summarises your offerings, and highlights key information with a convincing set of points as to why you should be appointed to the board. This will expand on the details you developed in your passenger profile and present your unique value proposition to the board.

In developing this, be sure to demonstrate your understanding of the board's roles and responsibilities, and organisational and operational context. Make sure you highlight the connection between the skills sought and what you have to offer. This is your opportunity to highlight how you can contribute as a good fit, both personally and professionally, to generate and deliver value for the organisation.

Part of your application, perhaps contained within or separate to the letter, will be your answers to any criteria requiring a response. This selection criteria are much like the measures used for assessing job applicants, however they differ for board work. Your attention to these details will need to be contextualised to the boardroom, outlining your capability and capacity to perform the role.

The types of questions, method of assessment, and expectations will also vary between the types of boards and organisations. In order to have the greatest impact, make sure you are specific and clear in your message.

Board CV

You will also develop what you might traditionally know as either a 'CV' or 'resume'. These words are often used interchangeably, however, they do actually have different meanings.

A resume is brief, often bullet pointed and typically one to two pages in length, with an emphasis on your work background. A resume includes a summary of your education, credentials, work history, skills, and possibly also a career overview.

A curriculum vitae (CV) is more academic in nature. It has a greater emphasis on academic information, experience and skills, and is generally longer (up to three pages). A CV contains details regarding qualifications, experience, awards and presentations, and any publications are also usually included.

Table 4 helps to explain and highlight these differences.

Format	Curriculum Vitae	Resume
Length	3+ pages	1 – 2 pages
Purpose	Factual background details	Tailored to the application
Focus	Professional experience	Work and employment
	Personal achievements	Professional experience
Contents	Contact details	Contact details
	Education	Education
	Employment	Employment
	Skills	Skills
	Membership	
	Publications	
	Presentations	
	Awards	

Table 4: CV and resume differences

Given that the nature of a board role is a strategic one, a CV for a board position is often requested. This is known as a 'Board CV'. A CV for a non-executive director role is also generally presented in a different format compared with CVs prepared for executive director roles. There are the standard contact details, industry affiliations, education and employment details; however, with a Board CV there is an increased focus on board and committee work, business operations, organisational experience, strategic planning and decision-making skills.

Board forms

In addition to your CV, letter and criteria, some boards or organisations require certain forms to be completed as part of the process. These may include formal nomination forms as well as consent forms for police checks or probity checks, for example. Some of these forms may require an endorsement or a witness signature, so make sure you find the right people you need for your application.

Given the different requirements indicated above, it is clear that application forms can vary a lot. They can also be unclear and confusing if you're not familiar with some of the terminology or what details they're asking for. If you're uncertain, you will not be alone so ask if you need help. It may seem tedious at times; however, these measures are a great example of good governance and it's important to become comfortable with this.

Board pitch

In some cases, depending on what you're applying for, you may be required to provide a candidate summary. This is generally used for online or hardcopy publications and promotions where board appointments are conducted via elections and voting. Much like State and Federal Government elections, local government and member-based organisations use this form of process for determining representatives for their board of decision-makers.

When it comes to providing a snapshot, you really want to hit the nail on the head so as to deliver your very best first impressions to your target audience. What do you bring to the board table? Why you? The profile you developed previously will help with preparing the summary. Just keep in mind, it's essential that your application is sincere.

Your application process may also involve a presentation. You may be required to put forward a verbal pitch or speech as part of your application. Face-to-face or video presentations are gaining momentum as demand for this format grows. If requested, use this opportunity to provide insight into you as a whole. In one simple pitch, show them who you are, personally and professionally … your overall brand.

Board applications

Your initial documentation (expression of interest, nomination, or application form) is likely to be forwarded digitally using email or an online platform, rather than submitted as a hardcopy. Get started early and give yourself plenty of time to collate your documents. Always be mindful of any closing dates. Some application processes have open timeframes until they've confirmed the right person for the vacancy.

Whilst the timeframe for submitting your documents might be known, the amount of time it takes to hear back may not be. It may take a number of weeks or even longer. In some circumstances, such as voting at an AGM, timeframes can be short and the result turnaround can be quick.

If you hear that you haven't been shortlisted or successful, request feedback on your application. The result may not be a reflection of you but rather other factors which have influenced the decision. You may have been deemed a good fit but another candidate may have been a better fit, given the skills presented and overall skills mix of the preferred board composition.

In any case, use your confidence and personal strength to seek and reflect on the feedback. This will only add to your experience and knowledge bank for your next board application. If finding a suitable board role takes longer than you expect, remain positive and engaged in being up-to-date with board and NED matters.

Even if you think you don't quite tick all the boxes or you think your chances are slim, be bold! Get out of your comfort zone. In the words of Napoleon:

> *Victory belongs to the most persevering.*
> – Napoleon Bonaparte,
> emperor of France

Give it a go! Especially if you have a strong gut feeling about an opportunity. Those responsible for the new appointment/s, whether it's the chair, board, executive or others, will look at your overall offer. Your value may be more than what was initially being sought. You may even be one of the few in the running for the role, as I was for my first board position.

I'm living proof of being bold and giving it a go! I saw a board position I was interested in and drawn to. I didn't think I had much of a chance as this was a sector-wide board and I was only junior relative to those who'd usually sat on the board. Not only that, it was also going to a member vote. Who would vote for me? What chance did I have? I was going up against leaders and senior executives in the industry in a democratic process!

You know the outcome: I got the gig and found myself working alongside CEOs and executive directors from the sector. I was a bucket of nerves in my first meeting but weirdly content. I was finally in a position where I was able to give all I had, both personally and professionally.

I no longer felt bored and unchallenged, but rather able to give everything by drawing on my broad knowledge and skills. Even better, I was able to contribute and make a difference to a sector responsible for local communities.

Application submission

I hope this chapter has not only helped you to prepare your flight documents but has demystified aspects of the application phase.

Whilst it may be overwhelming and appear heavy in administration, don't let it deter you from making progress toward that overall goal you have in mind. If you don't fancy yourself much of a writer or a presenter, yet you have all the other attributes of a great board member, seek help from a mentor or someone who can guide you.

With your package of flight documents sorted, there's only one more step before your flight: the shortlisting phase. Here, you'll be meeting with key people to further determine if you're the right person for the board, so preparation is essential.

Chapter 10 will guide you through this next step in preparation for your take-off!

Chapter 9 Checklist

- ☐ Process
- ☐ Documentation
- ☐ Application
- ☐ On to Chapter 10

10

BOARDING PASS

'Congratulations, you've been shortlisted!' You've just received your first endorsement as a suitable candidate for the board and are potentially on your way to getting your ticket to board.

You've made the cut for that board role you applied for. Well done! 'But what now?' you ask. This is a whole new world you may not have been a part of before and really want to join. It is slowly and steadily becoming a reality.

Take a moment to reflect on how much you've learnt so far since you first picked up this book. How much do you know now compared to when you started reading Chapter 1? A lot, I hope!

The only catch to getting your boarding pass is that you've got to ramp your efforts up again, proving yourself and convincing others that you fit their board.

In this chapter, we're going to cover the final steps involved in a board appointment process. This is the move to the big pitch phase and presenting yourself. The value here is that you will develop further confidence in what you may need to prepare for the interview process and any subsequent discussions.

The purpose of interviews, meetings and other discussions are to ascertain a greater understanding of who you are, what your values are, and how you relate with others.

You will be assessed for how you fit with the board and organisation, your ability to contribute, and your capability in decision-making. Even if you've arrived at this point through reputation or referral, you'll still be expected to meet with some or all of the board.

As a candidate and prospective member of a board, you'll be assessed according to the skills mix that the board is specifically looking for at that particular point. What they might look for this year might be different to what they looked for last time, or next time they need to fill a vacancy. Remember, smart boards are looking to balance alignment, skills, and diversity within their board composition.

Board interviews

The opportunity that awaits you as a shortlisted candidate has dual benefits. The interview or meeting not only provides the panellists with further insight into you and your offering, but it is also your opportunity to learn more about the board and organisation.

You can ask more specific questions about the board and the role which you hadn't been able to up until this point.

The meeting is also a good time to confirm if there's any limitations to you being able to fulfil the role which you weren't able to determine any earlier. Equally, if at any point along the way you are unable to continue with the process or fulfil the board role, politely advise the key point of contact.

What can you expect from meetings or interviews? They will often comprise the chair, members of the board, and potentially an executive of the organisation.

Sometimes an independent person may also be involved. In some instances, there may be four or more panellists, or even the full board meeting with you.

The interview or meeting may be held either at the organisation's head offices, a site office or another independent location. It may be either face-to-face, phone or even via video link. In my own experience, I've been involved in a range of interviews of varying formats.

The preferred process, whether the meeting is formal or informal, will be dictated by the type of organisation. The interview may include a series of set questions, or it may build on the application you submitted. Alternatively, it may be more of a casual discussion with key aspects targeted.

There are a range of key aspects you will need to address. You can expect those interviewing you will want you to highlight your views on the following (but certainly not limited to):

- Technical expertise and experience
- Business, finance and governance skills
- Organisation, sector and industry knowledge
- Values, perspective and approach
- Potential conflicts of interest.

Remember though, it may be different to a traditional job interview and you will need to focus on delivering your message in the context of boards, particularly in relation to the one you're applying for.

Interview preparation

Spend some time planning your pitch and performance. Some things to think about are:

- What do you want to communicate?
- How will you deliver your message?
- What will you wear?
- What might you need to take?

These considerations are equally as important for interviews via video as they are for face-to-face interviews. Think about what type of interview it is and who will be attending.

Consider also some of the questions you may want to ask of the interviewer or board. What haven't you been able to gain insight into so far in the process, or what might you wish to confirm about the role or other expectations?

Be sure to note the details of where you need to be and at what time. To help you get organised, make sure you correctly note the date, time and venue, and how you're going to get there. Simple stuff, but I've seen people get this wrong! Most importantly, be on time!

Potentially, as part of your meeting or interview, you could be requested to give a presentation. Make sure you know who will be there, what technology and facilities will be available to you, and how much time you will have. Be sure to share your individual style and allow the natural you to shine. This is the perfect opportunity for you to share the true you.

If you're in doubt of what to wear, always be presentable and professional. If you feel overdressed, don't worry. It's much better to be overdressed than underdressed! You'll want to feel confident.

One query that may arise following the interview may be the request for referees. Whilst some board members are likely to have quietly done their research on you, formal feedback from selected personnel often forms part of the process. Consider who may be suitable to advocate for you, again ideally in the context of board and NED work.

Post interview

Well done! Your interview and meeting went well, even though you may only be marginally happy with it. With so many questions in the interview, you might be feeling like you've been turned inside out and upside down.

You may think you didn't do so well. Careful not to be your own worst critic and judge yourself worse than you actually performed. There's no need to fall into the trap of self-doubt and underestimation. After all, two acronyms of 'FAIL' are 'First Attempt in Learning' and 'Forever Acquiring Important Lessons'! In fact, you've probably learnt a lot more than you knew before about the process, yourself, the organisation, and board as a whole.

At this point, there's not much more that you can do other than await a response. If you haven't heard back for a while after submitting your documentation or conducting your interview, just relax. You've put your best foot forward and there's no more that you could have done.

Equally, if you expected to hear back by a certain date and you haven't yet, don't be alarmed. Everyone gets busy and thrown off course from time to time and responses can sometimes take longer than expected. It may take a period of time before you receive some form of contact regarding the next step, or correspondence declining your application. Hopefully in the short-term you should at least receive a polite, 'Thank you for applying'.

To know how to wait is the great secret of success.
- Joseph de Maistre,
philosopher and diplomat

If you're not fortunate in progressing in the process, seek feedback as to why you may have been unsuccessful. Are there any learnings you can take away regarding your application, interview, or presentation?

Reflect on this. Think about your experience, what worked and what could be improved for next time. Put faith in the fact that the right opportunities will arrive at the right time.

This is potentially just the beginning of a whole new chapter for you. The fact that you have been through the process of assessing the suitability of an opportunity and applying, gives you substantial insight into this world which is new to you.

Patience creates confidence, decisiveness and a
rational outlook which eventually leads to success.
- Brian Adams,
journalist and author

Offer of directorship

Irrespective of the outcome, you've already benefitted from your new journey and experiences to date. You've undergone a massive transformation since having stepped into the world of boards – new knowledge, new understanding, new thinking, and new confidence. You've finally taken that leap towards the boardroom which you'd always dreamt about.

Your story could be like mine. In a daze, half asleep on a tropical island when you receive a phone call saying that you've been appointed. Or perhaps the next email you open will be a letter that says, *We are pleased to advise that your application has been successful, and you have been appointed to the board.*

Congratulations, you've been offered the job! You've received your ticket to board, which you've worked so hard to earn! You've proved yourself to be the right fit and best candidate for the role.

Imagine the sense of satisfaction, achievement, and excitement when you receive that news you've longed to hear? The news of that opportunity to rise up, draw on everything you've got, contribute to something new and meaningful, and be involved in something personally fulfilling. What a great sense of contentment. What a privilege to contribute as the decision-maker of an organisation.

When I received each of my board offers, they were in different formats, again reflecting the varying nature of the organisations and appointment procedures. I was advised about my appointment offers by phone calls and emails, followed by formal notifications.

There were letters and paperwork from Ministers delivered in the mail, emails from CEOs, and immediate determinations at AGMs.

When you become successful in receiving an acceptance or offer to join a board, realise that you have two options available to you. You are obviously open to accept the offer and move forward to boarding, but you may also choose to decline the offer if anything has changed since your initial application. Best then to try to catch the next flight.

Sometimes circumstances can change from the time of application to being offered a position. Perhaps health or personal reasons, a new job or maybe conflicts have arisen that will impact your ability to commit to accepting an offer. Maybe you landed another board or committee role, or maybe the organisation has morphed over that time, and it no longer aligns with your values.

There's no need to waste your time or that of others, if for legitimate reasons you decide against taking up the board position. Maintain your integrity by being honest and upfront, and politely decline.

I was personally in a situation once where I had to decline an offer of a board opportunity as a result of health reasons. Some circumstances can't be avoided but boards are not unreasonable, and they do not want anyone to commit who isn't in a position to do so.

If, however, you're still good to go, and this is right for both yourself and the board, seize it! Grab that opportunity and boarding pass with both hands and get to the check-in desk for your flight!

If the butterflies are churning in your stomach from nervousness as opposed to a bad feeling, my advice is to remember the words of world champion aerial skier Lydia Lassila: 'Face your fears and live your dreams!'

With this in mind, I want to share with you some other words of inspiration and advice, this time from mountaineer Brigitte Muir, an Australian woman who conquered Mt Everest in 1997. I was fortunate to meet Brigitte at an event I worked at many years ago, and she signed a copy of her book *Climbing Mount Everest* with the words 'Live your dreams'.

Between Lydia and Brigitte, there's a strong theme about conquering boundaries, climbing to new heights, living your vision, and doing what's true to you.

Take these wise words to heart and apply them in a way that drives you. There's no reason why you can't achieve such great heights either.

Ticket to board

In this chapter, we've explored possibly the hardest phase for you. You've stepped outside of your comfort zone and been put to the test. You passed with flying colours and even better, you've been offered an appointment, a seat at the board table.

In Chapter 11, we're going to outline what you can expect once you've boarded your flight. You'll find out what you'll need to know in your first few months and get some tips for settling into your new environment.

Chapter 10 Checklist

- ☐ Interview
- ☐ Impact
- ☐ Appointment
- ☐ On to Chapter 11

11

TAKE-OFF

Now you have your ticket and you are preparing for take-off!

You've endeavoured to understand the world of boards, learnt about the BoardSpectrum, researched organisations, investigated a vacancy, prepared your documentation, embarked on an application process, participated in an interview, and had subsequent discussions.

You impressed those assessing you so much they've given you your wings to fly. They've rewarded you with the opportunity you've been imagining for a long time. You set a goal, followed your heart, and achieved what you wanted.

> *Too many people measure how successful they are by how much money they make or the people that they associate with. In my opinion, true success should be measured by how happy you are.*
> *– Richard Branson,*
> *business magnate, philanthropist and author*

You now form part of a team which completes a matrix of different skills on a board and is charged with making decisions for the future. This achievement not only acknowledges your skills and experience but confirms your abilities and recognises your credibility in your field (as someone who can and will add value).

You are now officially a non-executive director and you're boarding your flight. Equipped with your case of skills, you've checked-in and you're stepping aboard to hear the announcement:

'Welcome! Your flight to the boardroom is now ready. Please have your boarding pass out. Please find your seat, sit down, buckle up and hold on! Prepare for take-off …'

In this chapter, you'll learn about what you need to know and what you need to do to ensure a smooth transition into your new role. I want to help you understand what to expect during the ascent of your flight and share how you can get up to speed without feeling overwhelmed.

That way you can gain further insight, understanding, and confidence around some of the more specific matters relating to your new adventure. Let's get you acclimatised so that you can settle in, be comfortable in performing your role, and fly higher.

Seat on the board

Your take-off will be steep. Most likely, you will have lot of questions and lots to absorb in the first few months – not just about being a new non-executive director and your new board but about the direction the organisation is heading in, what's going on and the intricacies of the business.

This will be a key phase where you will learn both formally and informally. As with any workplace, the boardroom will naturally provide a learning environment where you'll continue to develop throughout your board appointment.

Whether you're fresh to the space or have circled boardrooms a few times, you and all other board members will continue to gain something new. There's no need to think you're the only one who will be learning. Everyone has come from a different corner of knowledge and experience to be there and aren't necessarily familiar with all the different aspects of the board.

You may have any number of thoughts running through your mind. 'What do I do now?', 'What do I do next?', and maybe, 'I feel like a fraud!'

These are all pretty normal feelings and questions that many people experience when moving into something new. Let's not forget the steps you've taken, meetings you've had, and scrutiny you've been through. Remember you were judged the best person for the role.

We as humans have a tendency at times to underestimate ourselves. Referred to as the 'imposter syndrome', it is something many can relate to. A frame of mind where you don't feel worthy or justified to be fulfilling a certain role or set of responsibilities.

Although not an actual disorder, the term 'imposter syndrome' was coined by clinical psychologists Dr. Pauline Clance and Dr. Suzanne Imes in 1978. Clance and Imes found that despite having adequate external evidence of accomplishments, people with imposter syndrome remained convinced that they didn't deserve the success they had attained (Dalla-Camina, 2018).

Sometimes it can take a while to settle into a different routine or set of circumstances. Think about when you travel on a plane – it can take time to relax into your seat. From memory, I think it took me a good number of months in my first board role before I really felt settled.

Even many executives, entrepreneurs, employees, and business operators take a period of time to adjust to new roles and responsibilities. Think about a time in your life when you felt like this but eventually found your groove.

This initial phase on the board is just that – initiation. Sit back, relax, and soak up the atmosphere. Take this time to observe, learn and practise your communications to effectively contribute to the discussions, debate and decisions.

Introductions

First things first when you arrive at your boardroom destination, be sure to get a comprehensive induction and introduction to the board and organisation. These include the finer details about how the organisation functions, what governance is in place, and how your board will work together.

You can expect to learn greater detail about the various aspects of the organisation, particularly with respect to strategy, structure and systems, as well as plans, programs, and procedures.

At the very least you should expect to receive a raft of information, some of which you may have already seen during your research phase. These might include, and certainly not limited to, strategic plans, financial reports, and statements, governance documentation, expert reports, and key project updates.

Most importantly, your induction needs to include the necessary information you need to adequately bring you up-to-date regarding the board and your organisation, and its broader context.

The induction may be delivered in different formats, such as presentations, hardcopy information, soft copies, or online internal or external links to details. Presentations may be delivered by the chair, board members, CEO, executives, staff members, and/or other specialists or consultants.

Many boards are responsible for physical sites, including property, assets, and infrastructure. A part of your induction would ideally involve ground level, grassroots insights from the people and places you're dealing with. You'll gain a lot of knowledge from site visits where you can learn what is going on in your business and results of the strategic decisions to which you'll be contributing.

Even if your board has limited site responsibilities, talking with key staff is essential to further understanding how your business is operating and performing. When I was appointed to a board with major site responsibilities, I visited the site and met with various staff and stakeholders to gain a deeper understanding of the business for which I was now responsible for making decisions. It helped me gain insight into the issues and challenges of our operations but also what some of the positive approaches and outcomes were.

Important also, is taking the opportunity to bond with your fellow board members. Given the irregularity and the formality of board meetings, it can be difficult to appreciate each other's points of view without knowing a little more about each individual.

Everyone has their own unique life, often with fascinating stories to share. Get to know them as a whole person, their character and personality with their various hats on. Learn their interests and values, and the insights they bring to the table. What are their key skills, attributes or talents? What's important to them?

Board meetings

Regular board meetings will be set either by the chair or as agreed to by the board as the collective. The same applies to any subcommittees and meetings. Meeting dates are often, but not always, set well in advance to provide the greatest opportunity for board members to be available to attend.

The timing of meetings can be dictated by various events and organisational obligations. These can include key strategic activities of the business such as regulatory timeframes, AGMs, corporate planning processes, budget cycles and/or major projects. The exception is when a special or extraordinary meeting needs to be held – this can often happen at short notice.

Generally, board meetings will comprise the chair, deputy chair, and board members. The meetings may also be attended by the CEO, executive directors and other executives, managers and project leads, or external guests.

Guests or third parties are often invited to attend a board meeting but usually only for a short time. These people may be key staff, experts, specialists, consultants or perhaps even stakeholders, who may attend to present information to the board or discuss a particular issue. This provides an opportunity for all members of the board to listen, learn, ask questions, discuss, and comprehend the details around specific matters.

Plan well for your board meetings. Find out when they are and what format they take. Get those dates in your calendar to make sure you're available. Understand the pre-meeting process of setting the agenda and receiving and reviewing board papers.

Believe it or not, even in this digital age, many board and committee papers are still circulated in hardcopy! Be sure to read your papers when you receive them. This will provide you with sufficient time before meetings and outside of the boardroom to ask any further questions and formulate your own independent views for discussion.

Whilst you may be considered the go-to person in a particular area of expertise, as a board member you are expected to form a view on all matters. It is your duty and responsibility to ask whatever questions you need to assist you with this. You need to be satisfied that you have all the information required to process and progress the discussion, and to determine the options, outcomes and direction to be undertaken, as well as the actions that need to follow. See Figure 7 as a basic flow of board work.

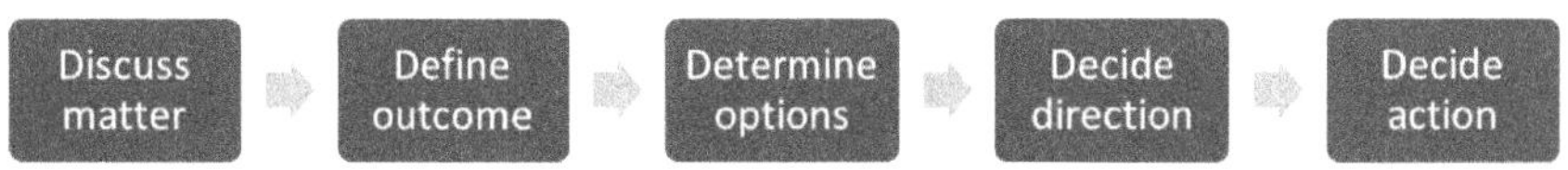

Figure 7: Flow of board work

Minutes are a record of notes from the board meeting outlining directions and decisions. They are considered to be an accurate and true record of the key points raised and the actions arising from the meeting. As a board member, one of your duties is to endorse minutes from the previous meeting. You are also obligated to maintain confidentiality when it comes to board matters and only disclose details agreed to by the board.

Settling in

During the initial stages, you may find you're feeling like an apprentice, but you're unlikely to get fired after your first meeting! Be mindful that everybody in the boardroom has an equal voice – just because you're the rookie, or maybe one of several rookies, it makes no difference. During your ascent, acclimatising can take time.

Remember, you've been appointed on your merit. Your opinion is as valid as anyone else's around the board table and collectively you bring a rich blend of insight for decision-making. Irrespective of age, gender, ability, culture, and years of technical or business experience, you have a set of attributes, points of view, and perspectives which are valuable.

Again, be bold! By asking the question, you'll discover new information helpful to not only yourself but those around the table who don't have the confidence to ask. Be sure your questions are understood and always clarify to get the answer you need.

There is no such thing as a dumb question.
- Carl Sagan,
scientist and author

Consume new information, absorb it like a sponge, ask lots of questions, and ponder what you hear and observe. You can only do your best along the way with the information you have available at the time. To consider matters and opportunities as they arise, make informed decisions and take steps in the right direction.

Part of your effective contribution will be drawing on your human/ soft skills and your level-headed capabilities. Leave those nerves behind so they don't interfere with your ability to think critically, analytically, creatively, and innovatively.

Acknowledged – the initial meeting on a new board can be daunting. You may also find yourself being the peer to people you never expected to be. When I first started on one of my boards, I had a very amusing time in my first meeting.

I had been appointed to a board with a gentleman who was well known for his work many years prior. He was the regular weatherman who I grew up watching on television. His voice was distinctive and his face easily recognisable. Not only was I entering my first board meeting on a new board as the only new member, but the seat saved for me happened to be next to him!

I had to pinch myself! It was quite surreal, sitting around a board table with someone I used to watch on TV as a child. Listening to this man's distinctive voice, I was waiting for him to break into, '… and looking at the week ahead for Melbourne. It's going to continue to be cold, wet and raining for the next five days'. It probably took me a year of meetings to stop waiting for him to talk about the weather!

During my board roles, I have also met and worked with other interesting people I didn't expect to meet, including:

- High profile business and community leaders
- Ministers and members of Parliament
- Specialist technical experts
- Leading consultants
- Passionate volunteers and change-makers.

Not only have these people helped to extend my knowledge base, but many remain colleagues and some I can even call friends.

Making progress

Boarding your flight and exploring new horizons is an exciting prospect. Over time, you will no doubt be presented with some interesting opportunities and things may not always go where you would expect. During my board roles, I was fortunate to get involved with many different projects and matters I couldn't have predicted.

Once you've acclimatised, you may seek opportunities to make improvements for your board and organisation. I did this. I identified additional areas for improvement beyond what was on the board's agenda.

I took the initiative to drive change and help streamline processes to ensure better governance. I worked with my chair, fellow board members, and executive colleagues to make improvements and updates to policies and procedures.

Hopefully this chapter has pulled together some essential insights and steps for you, key details for what it's like to be on a board, and what to expect when you first take-off on your board appointment.

The final chapter in this journey will explore some other aspects to further help you settle into your new role and develop good habits. Now that you've taken flight to the boardroom, we want you to … fly high at altitude without attitude!

Chapter 11 Checklist

- ☐ Inductions
- ☐ Discussions
- ☐ Decisions
- ☐ On to Chapter 12

12

FLYING HIGH

You know you're flying high when you hear, 'We've now reached our cruising altitude, so you're free to unbuckle and move around the cabin'.

What a relief! You can now really relax and enjoy the flight. The only problem with flying high is you can be at risk of slipping into autopilot and potentially entering a danger zone.

I'm referring to the danger zone of complacency. Be careful not to get too comfortable and lose your sense of direction or purpose. Equally, be prepared for any turbulence so you're able to adapt to changes in conditions, as there will be ups and downs and crosswinds pushing you in different directions.

Irrespective, in gaining greater height, you should now have a better view of this whole new world of opportunity. You will continue to develop both personally and professionally, advancing yourself as well as enhancing your board's performance. This final chapter aims to help you further realise your growth and opportunity.

Beyond the boardroom

This flying framework has taken you on a journey of self-discovery and transformation to unlock your personal potential. Your capabilities are now no longer a secret.

This journey you've embarked on may be lifelong and your elevation may continue to increase. Whilst following this blueprint has taken you to a destination you may have thought you couldn't get to, it may simply be a stopover in your board career or overall life travels.

Your commitment in reading this book (your time, energy, and resources) is a testament to your decision to invest in your future. This process of action, experience, and learning, will continually change you and propel you forward.

Throughout your journey to the boardroom and beyond, be sure to uphold the concept of lifelong learning to further build and update your knowledge and skill base. This doesn't necessarily mean getting new qualifications but rather refers to the concept of continually growing as a person, broadening your horizons, keeping abreast of societal or technological changes, and further connecting with your family, community or network.

Lifelong learning considers the full breadth of soft and hard skills that keeps you current, relevant, and up-to-date, and elevates you higher. Irrespective of your roles (volunteer or paid), such development helps maintain an open mind and happiness. Learning connects us and makes us feel good, mentally and emotionally, and contributes to having a good sense of purpose and confidence (Hartley, 2017).

Give thought to what future skills may be needed and what you can continually offer. There are a range of organisations researching and predicting the necessary skills to effectively work and function in the future, as noted in Chapter 4.

You may wish to undertake some informal or formal training to boost your knowledge. Whilst you don't have to panic and rush out to do the next course available, identifying gaps or opportunities is helpful to guide you and focus any future learning; some of which you may even attain throughout your board experience.

Self-reflection forms a very big part of self-development and success as a director. As explored in Chapter 5, a self-assessment can provide insight and help you fly higher. In enhancing yourself, you will also enhance the overall skill base of the broader board.

Perhaps there's still a little concerned voice saying, 'But what if I don't know everything even after six months?' Your role as a NED is a strategic role and at the very least you have taken steps seeking to understand matters, raised questions to be explored, and ensured issues are addressed. More importantly, what's notable is your commitment to a diligent approach and attempts to take action to deal with matters accordingly.

Transformation

Another option to help you is to get a coach or mentor who can guide you through your journey. Even though you've made it to the boardroom, make sure you find someone who has board experience to help guide you effectively. Be sure that they are suitable and trustworthy, and that they are someone you feel comfortable and open with. This relationship is an important one and you want to be able to approach them when you need to.

The time, effort, and commitment you make to a board is greatly valued by your fellow colleagues, your organisation, your stakeholders, and your community. Whilst you are focused on making a difference, you are also contributing to your own future, helping to make good future decisions for both the short and long-term.

The bonus is that over time you will continue to gain experience in the process of decision-making and good governance, underpinning yourself with fabulous skills to apply across other facets of life.

Board function and effectiveness are key to moving forward together in the same direction. Cruising collectively at altitude and further strengthening capability and capacity relies heavily on respectful communications and a healthy culture. The boardroom can be like an aeroplane cabin where confined spaces don't cope well with a lot of noise or big egos!

Given the role of the board is a high level strategic one for setting directions, it is important that it remains in this cruising zone at altitude. A good board will regularly check-in on their collective outcomes and individual director performances.

Remember, having a seat at the board table is a privilege. It is an opportunity that you not only identified as a goal in your own personal journey, but one you recognised for the benefit and value for others. You personally achieved what you perhaps thought you couldn't do, and also what others maybe thought you couldn't do!

Flying higher on a board is about continually bringing all that you've got to the role, not just in the meetings. I believe being a good non-executive director involves:

- Imagining possibilities
- Recognising opportunities
- Using your initiative
- Putting your best thoughts forward
- Contributing all you can
- Creating great outcomes.

No matter where you were on your journey, whether you were board-curious, board-interested, or board-experienced, I hope this book has helped you to:

- Determine why now is a great time to consider a board role, or your next one
- Understand your purpose and qualities better
- Develop self-belief and confidence
- Understand boards and committees better
- Appreciate what pathways to the boardroom best suit you
- Know how to find board opportunities
- Assess the suitability of board opportunities
- Know what you need and steps to take
- Know where to find more guidance and information.

This relatable blueprint process was aimed to inspire, empower, educate and transform your perception about boards, and to guide you to opportunities which you may only have imagined.

As you now look in the mirror, I hope it has opened your eyes to seeing something great – the new you!

The new you

At this stage, to complement your transformation, be sure to surround yourself with things that inspire you and make you feel good. This is not about indulgence or opulence, but a fulfilling and empowering sense of calm and confidence with presence and peace.

Surround yourself with inspiring people, read and listen to wise words, and care for yourself and others. Connect with what works for you.

To help you sustain this, prepare a poster for your wall. Something you will place where it will continually inspire you, not just daily but many times a day.

Choose whatever graphic or image most appeals to you and write words which light you up (maybe even your favourite quote).

Allow yourself to create something fun which reflects your personal vision. Use different colours and different fonts to spark your soul. Create what you want, how you want it, just for you.

There are no rules! Make as many copies as you wish and change it as often as you want to or need to. Keep it fresh, inspiring and empowering.

A new era

Your presence on a board is not just about physically getting your seat at the board table, but about being present in your body, mind, and heart. This is a real opportunity to work on optimising individual and collective performance when making decisions.

This is, in part, why I entitled my board and committee support business *Board Presence* – to reflect all that you and your colleagues can bring to the boardroom, and equally all that I can bring to help you.

To reflect this philosophy, I've developed the following guiding principles. These values help drive an approach where directors and boards of the future can thrive.

The success of individual directors and the board as a collective, depends on an alignment with the five key aspects I've highlighted in Figure 8.

These are five Fs that make up the *Board Presence* principles. I believe these are the minimum ingredients for directors and boards to achieve future sustainability and success.

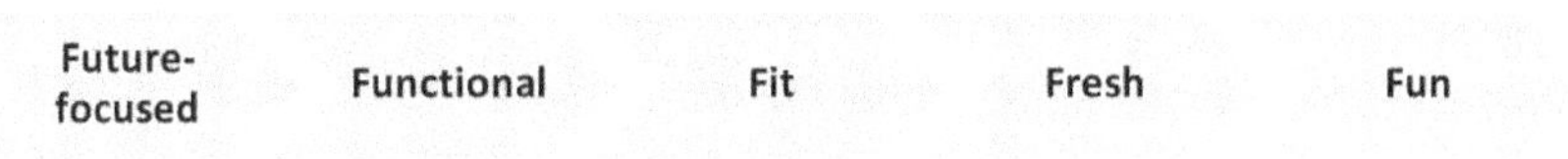

Figure 8: The Board Presence principles

To define and further explain the five Fs:

- Future-focused: Where the collective considers the long-term outcomes of their business, using the best available information to make sound judgements of social, environmental, and economic impacts and benefits.
- Functional: Where all members of the board or committee exercise respect for each other, both inside and outside of the boardroom, communicating collaboratively and collegiately, and efficiently address matters.
- Fit: Where all members of the board or committee are healthy in body, mind, and spirit, in order to take on information, process details, and exercise good decision-making to effectively fulfil their director duties.
- Fresh: Where the skills mix of the board is optimised and all members bring current, contemporary, and relevant perspectives to the board table.
- Fun: Where all members of the board are content and fulfilled by their board role, and the experience it brings personally and professionally.

Effective and successful boards are as simple as the right people, with the right skills, on the right board, for the right reasons, at the right time!

You've travelled so far. Well done! You embarked on this journey with some baby steps and have since taken significantly larger steps.

You've fulfilled a goal, gained greater self-fulfilment and now you're making a difference.

Perhaps for you the journey may have been confronting, challenging or even raw; yet hopefully it's been exciting, rewarding and satisfying!

It has been my pleasure to write this book for you. Taking flight with you has been an adventure. Thank you for joining me.

On board your flight and journey, you often won't know who you'll meet, who you'll sit next to, what's over the horizon or to what other destinations you will venture to. Whatever your pathway, celebrate your steps and your achievements as you go.

You did it! You're now on a board which has reinforced your value. Not only have you established a physical presence on a board, but you've also ensured your overall persona will positively influence the board. A powerful opportunity where you are able to be all you are, all you can be, contribute all you want, and make all the difference you wish.

I really hope that I have inspired you to continue to do what fills your heart so you can fill the hearts of others! Go ahead, put your best foot forward, find your untapped potential, and realise your dreams. Continue to cruise and fly high!

No matter your status or background, roles and careers within boards and committees are there waiting for you. You don't have to wait for one board role to finish before you seek or start the next.

You now have your wings and those wings will grow to take you to where you wish. Go forth and fly higher! Fly as high as you can go!

Until we meet again, give it all you've got. Fulfil your dreams. Make your journey meaningful. Make a difference!

You've got this!

Chapter 12 Checklist

- ☐ Continuous development
- ☐ Make a difference
- ☐ Celebrate!

AFTERWORD

I have truly enjoyed writing this book and I feel privileged that you have read it. It has been exciting and rewarding to have completed a book of over 40,000 words!

The idea for this book arose when I was regularly asked questions about getting on boards. Having worked on and with boards, I realised I had learnt so much from my own journey. I had developed a board career myself and had stories and insights I could share. While I'm not an ultimate expert, I am someone with proven experience who has sat on and contributed to various types of boards and committees for more than 15 years.

This book was written with the aim of giving you an introduction and to help guide you through the initial stages of considering board work.

My big *why* was to inspire, educate, and empower you to do something you're interested in and to help you take action. I wanted to demystify the world of boards and the journey associated with finding a board role.

I yearned to help you take control of your goal and break down any barriers holding you back. My aim was to not only help you develop personally throughout this process, but more specifically, to find that position in the boardroom. Even after all this, there's so much more I want to share with you.

Whether your board journey is a short or long one, you will grow as a person, developing over time with your extended knowledge, understanding and confidence. You will continue to morph and adapt to change as a result of your collective experiences and commitment to lifelong learning, all whilst making a difference.

The pathways and destinations you travel to in the future will be a result of the conscious effort you invest in your journey. I encourage you to listen to and follow both your heart and your gut.

I also encourage you to stick with your journey to the boardroom. Like any flight, there will be ups and downs but overall the trip can reach great heights. Remain connected to your purpose, your vision, and your goals. Take and enjoy one step at a time.

Your exposure to a range of people and experiences will enrich your perspectives. Your mind and your skills will continue to develop and evolve over time, forever creating a newer you!

Further insights and information are available for you on the Board Presence website at **www.boardpresence.com.au**. Here, you will find a range of resources and programs available to further guide and support you.

If you'd like to continue your flying journey to the board or fly faster, the accompanying *Fly to the Boardroom* online course is also accessible via the website (more details are included on the following page).

Once again, thank you and congratulations on reading *Fly to the Boardroom*! I wish you an amazing flight and wonderful travels!

Please contact me for more help via info@boardpresence.com.au and also to share your board journey and experiences. Also, please feel free to join the Board Presence communities on social media to connect with other like-minded people.

I'm pleased to have held your hand on this journey and I look forward to sharing more adventures with you!

Stacey

Fly to the Boardroom Course

Want to get on a board? Want to accelerate faster to the boardroom or fly higher?

Consider undertaking the online course accompanying this book, *Fly to the Boardroom*, accessible via the Board Presence website. The course builds on the book with greater information, reinforces what you've learnt, and makes it easier for you to reach the boardroom.

This comprehensive course includes:

- Structured modules to guide you through a framework for action
- Relevant information to help you with important steps
- Videos, infographics, and written content to give you clarity
- Links to supporting information to help extend your knowledge

- Tasks to help advance your understanding
- Worksheets to help you with your board journey
- Templates to help you prepare a board application
- Checklists to guide your progress

Throughout and upon completion of the course you will gain:

- More knowledge about boards
- A broader understanding of how to find suitable board opportunities
- Greater clarity of your personal board value
- Deeper insight into how to put your best foot forward
- The finer details for a board role application
- Help with planning your board career
- Greater confidence for the boardroom

In addition to the course, there is also the opportunity to gain personalised help including:

- Support throughout the course
- Feedback on your documentation
- Guidance on your application
- Mentoring and coaching

Further details, enrolments and/or bookings can be found at:

www.boardpresence.com.au

You can also subscribe via the website to receive further information and updates.

Glossary

A

Accountability: Accepting, having, or showing responsibility; either as an individual, group or organisation.

Accumulated: Growth or increase by continuous additions.

Administration: The process and activities required to operate an organisation.

Advisory: Providing specialist or expert recommendations without the authority to enforce them.

Annual General Meeting (AGM): A meeting which is held every 12 months and reports on organisational activities relating to the previous year and plans for the upcoming 12-month period.

Annual report: A document outlining the year's progress including activities, actions, and outcomes from the previous 12-month period.

Appointment: The formal act of allocating or assigning individuals to a specific role or position.

Assets: A person, property, possession, or financial holding that is considered a valuable resource with future benefit.

Australian Stock Exchange (ASX): The organisation which operates Australia's share market and a place for companies and investors to trade shares.

Authority: An organisation or other entity which has a particular role, responsibility and/or control over certain matters or jurisdictions.

B

Benefit: A good or advantageous outcome provided by someone, something, or a set of circumstances.

Board/Board of Directors: A formally appointed group of people responsible for overseeing the direction and the decision-making of an organisation.

Board career: The progression of the occupation, profession, and practice of board work throughout a stage of one's life.

Board Chair/Chairperson: The elected person who presides over the board, responsible for leading the board, its activities, and its meetings.

Board composition: The elements which make up a board.

Board papers: The documentation issued to board members for discussion and deliberation at a board meeting.

Board positions: The roles that make up a board.

Board subcommittee: A group of individuals or members, appointed to form a group, responsible for considering specific matters on behalf of the board.

Business model: A plan for the conduct and execution of a business, to viably sell products or deliver services.

C

Capability: The ability and provision of skill to undertake something to a certain standard or quality.

Capacity: The maximum amount that something can contain or produce; a person's ability to do something.

Chief Executive Officer (CEO): The elected officer at the highest level of the management structure, responsible for the organisation's operations.

Collective: A group of individuals which act together as a group.

Committee: A group of individuals appointed to form a group, that are collectively responsible for considering specific matters.

Company: A commercial business with a legally governed structure.

Compliance: The act of meeting or enforcing set rules, legislation, and/or standards.

Confidentiality: The act of keeping information private.

Constitution: A legal document which outlines how an entity will be established, with instructions regarding authority.

Contemporary: The current and present time.

Corporate: Relating to a large company or group which acts as a single entity.

Culture: The interactions and behaviours commonly shared amongst a group, which reflects their beliefs, values, attitudes, and customs.

D

Decision-maker: One who assesses, analyses, and evaluates information, and participates in discussion to form an opinion that can be actioned.

Deliberation: Discussions which are carefully considered and often continue for a period of time.

Deputy: A person appointed as a substitute to act in or undertake the duties of a more superior position.

Digital disruption: The changes and advances in technology, which impact the value proposition of products and services.

Diligent: Conscientious, careful, and consistent effort in undertaking work.

Directorship: Describes the appointment of a director to a board.

Diversity: Describes a range of individual differences such as characteristics, attributes, and preferences.

E

Emotional intelligence: One's awareness and ability to control their feelings, responses, and interactions.

Entity: A business or other organisation.

Environment: The elements and space making up the natural, physical world including air, water, soil, animals, fungi, and plants.

Ethics/Ethical: The moral principles and behaviours which are generally considered to be acceptable, right, and good.

F

Federal Government: The nationally constituted parliamentary system which oversees national matters, also known as the Commonwealth of Australia or the Australian Government.

Financial capital: The monetary value of funds, materials, and/or assets.

For-profit: A commercial business structure or model with the primary intent of generating financial returns for monetary gain.

Functional: The ability to work properly for its intended purpose.

G

Gap analysis: A process of assessment and evaluation to determine deficiencies.

H

Human capital: The overall value of the individual human being, taking into consideration skills, attributes, qualities, and characteristics.

I

Ideation: The development of concepts and ideas.

Implementation: The process of introducing, or acting on, a plan or decision.

Incorporated organisation: A legal entity, group, or organisation, which is often categorised as not-for-profit. It can trade and can enter into contracts and agreements.

Independent: Free of external factors, influences, or dependencies.

Induction: A process of introducing someone to something new, providing information and details to assist in their understanding.

Industry: The work associated with activities and transactions of particular goods or services.

Infrastructure: The physical or organisational elements that are required for the operation of a society or enterprise.

Initiative: Acting on independent, new, or fresh thinking, approaches, and practices.

Instruments of appointment: A document which formalises the appointment of members, and outlines the relevant terms and conditions.

Intergenerational: Describing or pertaining to several family generations.

J

Jurisdiction: The power or right to exercise authority over a person, matter, or territory.

L

Legislation: The collective term for laws.

Legislative reform: The careful review and consideration of existing laws, usually with a view to implement changes to the legal system that will improve outcomes.

Local government: In Australia, this is known as the public administration authority (often referred to as a Council) that is responsible for community and municipal services within a designated area.

M

Matter: A topic, issue, or situation that is considered through discussions, deliberations, or a decision-making process.

Mentoring: The act of helping, guiding, or advising others with lesser experience.

Minutes: The set of notes taken during a meeting which contains details relating to key points of discussion, decisions made, and actions to be taken.

Moral: The concept of good, right, and acceptable behaviour, principles, and standards.

N

Natural capital: The value of natural environmental assets including rock, soil, water, air, and biodiversity.

Non-executive director: An elected member of a board with decision-making responsibilities.

O

Obligations: Duties imposed legally or morally on a person, group, or organisation.

Operational: Pertaining to the act of co-ordinating, managing, or making use of personnel, resources, and systems to deliver products and/or services.

Organisation: A structured group or business established for a particular purpose.

Outcomes: The positive or negative consequences, or results of actions undertaken.

Oversight: Specific to this publication, this term refers to the act of caring, giving attention to, and/or supervising.

P

Peak body: An organisation which represents an industry, sector, or community segment.

Performance: The act or process of undertaking and delivering a specified task or function, and the level of quality associated with its fulfilment.

Policy: An organisational document outlining specific directions, principles, and instructions which focuses on guiding conduct and courses of action.

Portfolio career: A career involving a diversified series of casual or part-time jobs, as opposed to a single full-time job.

Private industry: Businesses and organisations owned and operated by individuals or institutions.

Productivity: The level of organisational efficiency and production of goods and/or services, which is based on the effective application and use of resources.

Public sector: Organisations, groups, and government entities that provide public and community services.

Q

Qualifiers: Criteria which determine eligibility.

R

Rates of return: The financial, social, and/or environmental benefits gained from funding, resources, and/or effort.

Regulations: Directives or official rules made by government or authorities which can be enforced.

Representation: Speaking, acting, or advocating on behalf of another person or organisation.

Responsibility: A legal, appointed, or moral duty to take control of, manage, care for, or co-ordinate something.

Risk: The potential for adverse impacts, including loss, or harm, to people and/or property.

Royal Commission: The term which, in Australia, describes the highest form of investigation into important public matters.

Rules: A set of guiding principles, instructions, or directions regarding a specific activity.

S

Sector: A section of industry which delivers defined goods and/or services.

Social: Pertaining to humanity, communities, and society.

Social enterprise: An organisation focused on optimising environmental, social, and community benefits.

Stakeholders: Individuals, groups, or organisations who are connected to, or associated with, a project or purpose in which they have an interest.

Start up: A business or organisation in its infancy.

Statutory authority: An entity formally appointed with the responsibility of enacting legislation on behalf of the government.

Strategic plan: A formal business or organisational document containing the desired vision, objectives and goals, and steps on how to achieve them.

Sustainable: The ability to carry out activities, on an on-going basis, without compromising or degrading financial position, social quality, and environmental health.

T

Term of appointment: The contractually defined period of time in which a member is appointed to a board.

Transparency: Open and honest communication and conduct.

V

Values: A set of principles and beliefs.

Viability: The capacity to survive, thrive, and be successful, practical, and/or workable.

Vision: Inspirational ideas forming the desired goals for the mid to long term future.

References

AICD. (2019, December 19). *ASX hits 30% women on boards.* Retrieved December 19, 2019, from Australian Institute of Company Directors: https://bit.ly/2V1HawO

ASX Corporate Governance Council. (2019, February 1). *Corporate Governance Principles and Recommendations*, 4th Edition. Retrieved April 22, 2019, from https://bit.ly/38C2WLr

Australian Government. (2001, June 28). *Corporations Act 2001*. Retrieved April 22, 2019, from Federal Register of Legislation: https://bit.ly/39ECdxV

Bennett, T. (2013, March 11). Retrieved September 9, 2019, from Ty Bennett: https://bit.ly/2OZMbCc

Cambridge University Press. (2019). Definition 'Board'. Retrieved May 11, 2019, from Cambridge Dictionary: https://bit.ly/325lOje

Chen, S. (2014, March 4). *What are the stages of a business lifecycle and its challenges?* Retrieved April 16, 2019, from B2B Community: https://bit.ly/2OZiSzl

Cocorocchia, C. (2018, February 6). *Forget IQ. Digital intelligence will be what matters in the future*. Retrieved November 16, 2018, from World Economic Forum: https://bit.ly/2SNCDLy

Dalla-Camina, M. (2018, September 3). *The Reality of Imposter Syndrome*. Retrieved June 5, 2019, from Psychology Today: https://bit.ly/2V26jau

Delosa, J. (2014). *Unprofessional*. (John Wiley & Sons) Milton.

Delosa, J. (2016). *Unwritten*. (The Entourage Publishing) Sydney.

Edelman, (2020, January 19). Edelman *Trust Barometer 2020, Executive Summary*. Retrieved March 3, 2020, from Edelman: https://bit.ly/2U8SPaI

Edelman, (2020, January 19). Edelman *Trust Barometer 2020, Global Report*. Retrieved March 3, 2020, from Edelman: https://bit.ly/2U1SesT

Evan, C. (2016, July 28). *The 5 Essential Qualities of a Non-Executive Director*. Retrieved March 19, 2019, from The Chartered Governance Institute: https://bit.ly/38C4iWx

GIA. (2019, April). *What is governance?* Retrieved May 11, 2019, from Governance Institute of Australia: https://bit.ly/2wt1iO9

Gibbons, S. (2018, June 19). *You And Your Business Have 7 Seconds To Make A First Impression: Here's How To Succeed*. Retrieved May 11, 2019, from Forbes Media: https://bit.ly/2Hzt0Lm

Gillies, J., & Leblanc, R. (2005). *Inside the Boardroom*. (John Wiley & Sons) Ontario.

Goodman, A., Martin, M., & O'Kelley, R. (2018, December 30). *2019 Global & Regional Trends in Corporate Governance*. Retrieved April 22, 2019, from Harvard Law School: https://bit.ly/323gwow

Hartley, J. (2017, May 15). *Why Being an Adult Learner Improves Your Quality of Life*. Retrieved June 5, 2019, from Open Colleges: https://bit.ly/2P2cKqh

Koumouli, E. (2018, May 14). *The multifarious benefits of a diverse boardroom*. Retrieved March 24, 2019, from World Finance: https://bit.ly/2V1aXFC

Life. (2015, October 28). *Johari Window – Developing Self Awareness*. (T. L. Centre, Compiler) Retrieved April 26, 2019, from Life Coaching Centre: https://bit.ly/2OX0SWz

Macquarie University. (1997). *The Maquarie Dictionary, 3rd Edition*. (The Maquarie Library) Sydney.

McKinsey & Company. (2018, January). *Delivering through Diversity*. Retrieved March 23, 2019, from McKinsey: https://mck.co/3bQQWI7

Price, J. (2017, April 4). *Lack of financial records linked to company failure*. Retrieved April 16, 2019, from Australian Securities and Investments Commission: https://bit.ly/2UYON75

Sinek, S. (2009). *Start with Why*. (Penguin Group) New York.

Wilson, C. (2018, June 14). *Trusting Your Gut Is The Best Business Tool You've Got – If You Can Listen*. Retrieved April 26, 2019, from Forbes Media: https://bit.ly/323THku

World Economic Forum. (2018, September 17). *The Future of Jobs Report 2018*. Retrieved November 16, 2018, from World Economic Forum: https://bit.ly/2P4bfrH

Full reference links are available via the Board Presence website.

Acknowledgements

My most sincere thanks go to the following people for their contribution to making this book happen:

My husband, for his patience whilst I dived into writing this book and his support, reading the drafts and providing feedback.

My children, for their patience, encouragement, and support to complete this project.

Helen and Ivor Edwards, for reviewing the initial draft and providing me with essential guidance.

Arianne Rose, for reading the draft and providing a foreword at the front of this book.

Michael O'Brien, for reviewing the draft and providing me with helpful comments.

Dr. Susan Maastricht, for reviewing the draft and providing her thoughts.

Bruce Hemburrow, for providing a copy of the photo for the front cover of this book.

Linda Bester of Moonah Press, for her insight into graphics, content, books and the publishing journey, and for reviewing the draft and providing feedback.

Busybird Publishing, for their guidance and support in bringing this book to life.

ABOUT THE AUTHOR

Stacey Daniel was born in Melbourne, Australia. She always enjoyed writing as a form of expression and dreamt of one day writing a book to prompt deep thoughts and enrich discussions.

Stacey holds engineering and business qualifications and has worked across a range of industries and sectors on sites

of both state and national significance. After graduating university, her early work was in the mining industry in Kalgoorlie, Western Australia. Following on from this, she worked in local government in Victoria and, later, consulting nationally before starting her own business.

A natural educator and guide, Stacey has a passion for making things better and likes to create the best out of everything. During university she took up a sports coaching role (instead of doing the sport herself) due to the greater sense of satisfaction in helping others achieve their goals. After university, Stacey was inspired by the opportunity of one day becoming a non-executive director on a board, to contribute to good decision-making and generating sustainable outcomes.

Stacey has served on statutory authority boards, a peak industry board, and not-for-profit and community boards. At the age of thirty and very pregnant with her first child, Stacey was appointed to her first board role. Fifteen years later, she is sitting on her tenth board/committee, having accumulated around eighteen years of combined board work. She continues to serve and contribute as a member on various assessment and judging panels.

Adventures of all sorts form part of Stacey's life. Before children, she travelled overseas throughout Europe, Asia, America, Canada and New Zealand to experience the world. Yet the most transformational journey of them all was becoming a parent to two children and extensively exploring Australia with her young family.

As an entrepreneur, Stacey now focuses her energy on helping others as a Board specialist. She established her business Board Presence to support boards, committees, directors, and executives with better decisions for a better future.

Fly to the Boardroom is Stacey's first book. She continuously strives to help others, drive positive change and deliver great results.